Boot Camp for Leaders in K–12 Education: Continuous Improvement

Also available from ASQ Quality Press:

Permission to Forget: And Nine Other Root Causes of America's Frustration with Education
Lee Jenkins

Improving Student Learning: Applying Deming's Quality Principles in the Classroom, Second Edition
Lee Jenkins

The Principal's Leadership Counts!: Launch a Baldrige-Based Quality School
Margaret A. Byrnes with Jeanne C. Baxter

Insights to Performance Excellence 2006: An Inside Look at the 2006 Baldrige Award Criteria
Mark L. Blazey

Quality Across the Curriculum: Integrating Quality Tools and PDSA with Standards
Jay Marino and Ann Haggerty Raines

Thinking Tools for Kids: An Activity Book for Classroom Learning
Barbara A. Cleary, PhD and Sally J. Duncan

Smart Teaching: Using Brain Research and Data to Continuously Improve Learning
Ronald J. Fitzgerald

Continuous Improvement in the Primary Classroom: Language Arts
Karen Fauss

Continuous Improvement in the History/Social Science Classroom
Shelly Carson

Tools and Techniques to Inspire Classroom Learning
Barbara A. Cleary, PhD and Sally J. Duncan

Continuous Improvement in the Science Classroom
Jeffrey Burgard

Continuous Improvement in the Mathematics Classroom
Carolyn Ayres

There Is Another Way!: Launch a Baldrige-Based Quality Classroom
Margaret A. Byrnes with Jeanne C. Baxter

To request a complimentary catalog of ASQ Quality Press publications, call 800-248-1946, or visit our Web site at http://qualitypress.asq.org.

Boot Camp for Leaders in K–12 Education: Continuous Improvement

Lee Jenkins, Lloyd O. Roettger,
and Caroline Roettger

ASQ Quality Press
Milwaukee, Wisconsin

American Society for Quality, Quality Press, Milwaukee 53203
© 2007 by ASQ
All rights reserved. Published 2006
Printed in the United States of America
12 11 10 09 08 07 06   5 4 3 2 1

Library of Congress Cataloging-in-Publication Data

Jenkins, Lee.
  Boot camp for leaders in K–12 education : continuous improvement / Lee Jenkins,
Lloyd O. Roettger, and Caroline Roettger.
    p. cm.
  Includes bibliographical references and index.
  ISBN-13: 978-0-87389-681-8 (soft cover : alk. paper)
  ISBN-10: 0-87389-681-5 (soft cover : alk. paper)
    1. School improvement programs—United States. 2. Total quality management—
United States. 3. Educational leadership—United States. I. Roettger, Lloyd O.
II. Roettger, Caroline. III. Title.

  LB2822.82.J458 2006
  371.2—dc22   2006022499

ISBN-13: 978-0-87389-681-8
ISBN-10: 0-87389-681-5

Publisher: William A. Tony
Acquisitions Editor: Matt T. Meinholz
Project Editor: Paul O'Mara
Production Administrator: Randall Benson

ASQ Mission: The American Society for Quality advances individual, organizational,
and community excellence worldwide through learning, quality improvement, and
knowledge exchange.

Attention Bookstores, Wholesalers, Schools and Corporations: ASQ Quality Press
books, videotapes, audiotapes, and software are available at quantity discounts with
bulk purchases for business, educational, or instructional use. For information,
please contact ASQ Quality Press at 800-248-1946, or write to ASQ Quality Press,
P.O. Box 3005, Milwaukee, WI 53201-3005.

To place orders or to request a free copy of the ASQ Quality Press Publications
Catalog, including ASQ membership information, call 800-248-1946. Visit our
Web site at www.asq.org or http://qualitypress.asq.org.

Printed in the United States of America

♾ Printed on acid-free paper

Quality Press
600 N. Plankinton Avenue
Milwaukee, Wisconsin 53203
Call toll free 800-248-1946
Fax 414-272-1734
www.asq.org
http://qualitypress.asq.org
http://standardsgroup.asq.org
E-mail: authors@asq.org

Table of Contents

Part I Understanding the Fundamentals for Excellence

Part II   Tying the Fundamentals Together

Preface

*B*oot Camp? What experienced, well-educated leader would want a book with the title *Boot Camp for Leaders in K–12 Education* to be visible in his or her office? Such a title must indicate that the intended audience is aspiring leaders.

Not so. Our intended audience is all school leaders: those in the classroom and those whose professional life's mission is assisting those in the classroom. Then why the title?

It is because most of us are novices at leading schools where continuous improvement is the cultural norm. A culture in which all-time-bests are continually strived for, achieved, and celebrated is rare indeed.

Lee wrote *Improving Student Learning* to describe how continuous improvement looks in the classroom. Further, he edited the Continuous Improvement series written by four classroom teachers: Ayres, Burgard, Carson, and Fauss. He then described in *Permission to Forget* the root causes of educational frustration—the issues that make continuous improvement so difficult. Now, Lee is collaborating with Lloyd and Caroline Roettger to write the leadership companion.

Just how do leaders go about creating a culture of continuous improvement with administrators, teachers, support staff, parents, and students? *Boot Camp* is the right title; it communicates that in many regards education must start over. And that education is about "getting better," not about winning.

Introduction

A couple of notes: one to those who lead the nation's K–12 schools and one to those who train educational leaders (our fellow educational administration professors and school improvement consultants).

EDUCATION LEADERS

In a sense, this book began because of a conversation between the three of us. The conversation revolved around how each of us had been repeatedly asked the questions "How do you lead educators in the implementation of the LtoJ process to achieve continuous improvement?" and "How do Deming's quality principles and the Baldrige education criteria for excellence fit into our school improvement planning?" After a discussion, we had a series of answers, ideas, processes, and more questions that soon became the outline of this book.

With each of us having been educational administrators for many years, we quickly decided that any book we wrote should be written for practitioners. That is, it should be direct, to the point, and brief. In addition, it should provide reliable strategies and useful tools, and include connections to the Baldrige criteria, identify core values, and provide a set of guiding questions for self-assessment of the processes and system used for school improvement. Finally, we believed the book should offer various resources, provide a reading list of helpful books and articles, and be an easy read. It is our hope that you will find many solutions to the problems and challenges that you encounter as you work toward achieving excellence.

EDUCATIONAL LEADERSHIP PROFESSORS

When Caroline and Lloyd searched for texts to use in their classes, such as an educational administration introduction or survey course, a leadership course, a continuous improvement seminar, or a school improvement workshop for administrators, they could not locate a reasonably priced book that was easy to read and could be used by practitioners as a resource or guide for leadership, school improvement, and continuous improvement. As a result, we decided to create this book to meet those needs.

Because all three of us have been professors of educational leadership and educational administrators for many years, we chose to write a dual-purpose book: one that could be used by both school leadership professors and school leaders. We wanted the book to be one that our students would keep in their personal library instead of selling it back to the bookstore. We decided the book should be direct, to the point, and brief. In addition, it should provide reliable strategies and useful tools, and include connections to the Baldrige criteria, identify core values, and provide a set of guiding questions for self-assessment of the processes and system used for school improvement. Finally, we believed the book should offer various resources, provide a reading list of helpful books and articles, and be an easy read. It is our hope that you will find it a valuable tool to help train great future school leaders. If you choose to use this text in your class, we will be happy to participate in online or email discussions with your students. Contact Dr. Lee Jenkins at Lee@LtoJConsulting.com, Dr. Caroline Roettger at Caroline@LtoJConsulting.com, and Dr. Lloyd Roettger at Lloyd@LtoJConsulting.com.

Part I

Understanding the Fundamentals for Excellence

1

Aim: Defining the Target

The aim of this book is to assist leaders as they create a culture of all-time-bests when obstacles seem so overwhelming that educators are tempted to despair. It is the job of the leader to lead in such a way that the school or school district can always document improvement over the past. We call these improvements the all-time-bests.

School leaders are not taught how to establish a culture of all-time-bests. There are hundreds of books on leadership any reader could purchase other than this book, but the focus of this book is how leaders can create this culture of all-time-bests. Within this culture, the school and district know that improvement occurred, know what they did to improve, and know how to repeat the improvement, and the staff knows how much administrators and board members appreciate this improvement. The employees work in a culture where all-time-bests are the norm. They know that every little improvement is valued, because year after year of little improvements adds up to huge improvement.

Examples of all-time-bests include:

1. Least number of minutes wasted because of late buses. Best day ever.

2. Least number of dollars spent on dumpster emptying (waste management) per child. Best year ever.

3. The most correct responses on the random quizzes in a subject area per child, per class, or per school. Best student learning week ever.

4. Highest writing score ever (calculated by adding up total rubric scores for all students in school). Best writing sample ever.

5. Highest number of students scoring 3 or higher on one or more AP exams. Best year ever.

6. Least number of office referrals for discipline. Best week ever.

The regular celebration of all-time-bests will not occur in schools and school districts unless there is a clear aim to do so. In the rest of this chapter, we provide details to assist leaders in establishing their school or school district aim. We would hope that readers will not focus on the six all-time-best examples or even ways that they could celebrate an all-time-best in their school or school system. We would hope that readers will take the longer path of changing the whole school culture. When the culture changes, everyone will know it is their job to continually, forever, improve.

Establishing an aim that shouts out commitment to always do better is step one. There are many implementation steps after the aim is established, and thus, our book has more than one chapter. First, however, is the establishment of the aim.

An aim is written to communicate to both employees and customers what an organization is about. The aim sets the stage for future direction and decisions. It can be all-encompassing and powerful.

An example of a poor aim is *create lifelong learners*. Why is this so poor? Don't schools want to help create lifelong learners? The problems with *create lifelong learners* are (1) students come to kindergarten already programmed to be lifelong learners, and (2) the organization can never know if it ever achieved its aim. The students are younger than the staff, so the teachers and administrators are all expected to be dead before the students live out their lives and it can be determined if they were lifelong learners. The major problem with *lifelong learners* is that it creates no engine for improvement. It does nothing for students, staff, or parents. The aim of an organization must communicate improvement as a central tenet; otherwise, an aim is not needed.

Many state laws require teachers to meet with their principal in the fall and agree on annual objectives. In the spring, the two meet again to see if the goal was met. Goals from one year may have nothing to do with the next year or any other year. Each year stands alone. With an aim of all-time-bests, the annual objective meeting is not a meeting concerning merely what my objective is, but a meeting of what I am going to try out this year in order to do even better than before.

AIM OVERVIEW

The aim is one of the seven components of any system. A system is not complete without each of the seven elements: aim, customers, suppliers, input, process, output, and quality metrics. Any organization that is missing any element is not a system, only a collection of disparate parts. As a result, the first characteristic of a system is that it has a clearly defined and articulated aim. Absent an aim, there is no system.

Building the aim requires asking and answering two critical questions: What is this organization about? and What is it we're trying to do? As each of these questions are answered, the clarification of the answers can be accomplished by asking the follow-up questions, Why? Why? Why? Why? Why? at least five times. See Figure 1.1. This technique, as taught to us by Japanese quality experts, allows us to pursue a deeper understanding of the purpose, premises, and principles of the organization. Additional necessary questions include: What will it take to accomplish the aim? Will the customers care about the aim? On what basis do we hold onto the beliefs and assumptions that resulted in this aim? What data support this aim? and Where do our data come from? Again, ask Why? Why? Why? Why? Why?

Vision, mission, beliefs, and philosophy are all rings on the organizational target; the aim is the bulls-eye (Figure 1.2).

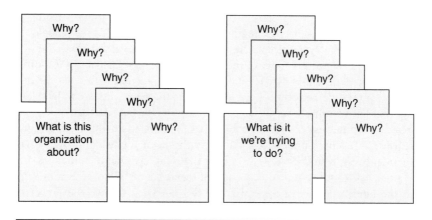

Figure 1.1 Getting to the root cause.

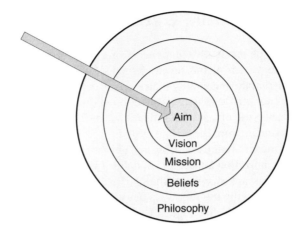

Figure 1.2   The aim is the school's purpose.

AIM HISTORY

Dr. W. Edwards Deming offered his aim for education in 1992 as "Increase the positives and decrease the negatives so that all keep their yearning for learning" (Deming 1992). In many respects it is most difficult to improve upon this aim. Surely, schools would not be anything like they are today if 13 years after beginning school students were as excited about learning as they were in kindergarten. Imagine the learning that could take place if all incoming geometry students were still in love with mathematics.

Lee was superintendent of the Enterprise School District in Redding, California. The school district staff and board wrestled with what the district's aim should be for a couple years. Since there was a good understanding that Dr. Deming's aim was probably all that was needed, the issue was how to communicate with the public that the aim was enthusiasm and not learning. Teachers understood that if enthusiasm for learning was high, then learning would occur. But school districts have many audiences and it wasn't difficult to envision a sour editorial page if Deming's aim went to the board for formal approval. We did not wish to lose the power of his idea, however, so the final outcome was "Maintain enthusiasm while increasing learning."

A limitation of "Maintain enthusiasm while increasing learning" is that it speaks only to instruction and not to all aspects of schooling, which include safety, discipline, attendance, finance, operations, and personnel. Thus, current thought regarding aim is merely "Increase success and decrease failure." Every employee in a school district can contribute to the increase of success and decrease of failure. For example, the job of a high school counselor is to increase success as measured by graduation rates, scholarships, AP credit, extracurricular participation, and so on. Failure is easier to measure—it is F's and dropouts. We realize that counselors also must respond to emergencies, but their aim should be what drives their efforts day to day.

We are not advocating that school systems adopt any of the aims listed here, but that they come to a consensus regarding their aim. It must be both short and profound—so people in large organizations can remember and take action.

ACTION STEPS

The first step in creating a school or system aim is to analyze current documents. Do these documents attempt to describe educational *heaven* or do they communicate a determination to improve? It may be appropriate to leave the vision, mission, and belief statements as they are but create an aim from these documents that succinctly describes the passion for creating the vision. This passion includes the desire to be held publicly accountable for making annual strides toward the perfection described in the vision, mission, and belief statements.

In this book, we provide many tools and concepts designed to assist leaders in all aspects of leadership. They are included with one purpose in mind: to assist leaders as they create cultures of all-time-bests.

Throughout the book, we will insert pertinent quotes from the Baldrige Criteria. Most school leaders who use the Baldrige Criteria as a guide subscribe to a philosophy of continuous improvement. Thus connecting our advice to the Baldrige language should not only help school leaders, but save considerable time.

Core Value

Organizational and personal learning that is directed not only toward better educational programs and services but also toward being more flexible, adaptive, and responsive to the needs of students and stakeholders.

Baldrige Connection

Describe how school leaders guide and sustain your school. Describe how school leaders communicate with faculty and staff and encourage high performance.

Guiding Questions

How do school leaders set organizational vision and values? How do school leaders deploy your school's vision and values through your leadership system to all faculty and staff, to key suppliers and partners, and to students and stakeholders, as appropriate? How do their personal actions reflect a commitment to the school's values?

Adapted from *2005 Education Criteria for Performance Excellence.*

RESOURCES AND READING LIST

Deming, W. Edwards. January 1992. American Association of School
    Administrators Conference. Washington, DC.
Jenkins, Lee. 2003. *Improving Student Learning: Applying Deming's
    Quality Principles in Classrooms,* 2nd ed., Chapter 1. Milwaukee:
    ASQ Quality Press.
Jenkins, Lee. 2004. *Permission to Forget: And Nine Other Root Causes of
    America's Frustration with Education,* Chapter 7. Milwaukee: ASQ
    Quality Press.
Scholtes, Peter R. 1998. *The Leader's Handbook: Making Things Happen,
    Getting Things Done,* Chapter 7. New York: McGraw-Hill.

2

Team: The Vehicle for Getting There

OVERVIEW

Leaders often espouse teamwork. They pronounce that we are a team and even purchase framed teamwork slogans. However, leaders often do not manage for teamwork. Why?

They do not understand the ideas of Deming's (1994) four generations of management, from least effective to most effective. The least effective management style is *I'll do it myself.* These hardworking people never delegate anything important, work 12-hour days, half the weekend, and are very defensive whenever somebody suggests improvement: *Don't they realize how hard I'm working?* The second-generation leader is what people imagine, or remember, from boot camp: *Do it exactly as I say.* The clear message is *leave your brain at home* and do it my way. Everyone knows that the *highway* is the only alternative. Unfortunately, many leaders who have rejected one and two have landed on three: *What gets inspected, gets done.* Everybody is evaluated on their ability to meet individual goals. They have been instructed that management by objectives (MBO) is the ultimate leadership style; they have been wrongly instructed. Consider an automotive industry example: the engine leaders met their goals, so did the transmission people, and even the drive train department succeeded; however, the car doesn't run. MBO assumes that if everybody did their best and met their goals, the organization would be perfect (Roettger 2000). Nothing could be further from the truth. Everyone knows that a superb meal is far more than the sum of its ingredients.

According to Deming (1994), generation-four management is the ultimate in leadership. The first step is agreement on an aim. That is why this book is organized with aim as the first chapter. If people who share responsibility for an organization disagree on the purpose of the organization, teamwork will be only the clichés framed on the meeting room walls. Once a group of employees has agreed on the aim, the leader has the responsibility to manage in such a way that people gain their joy from the team's success. See Figure 2.1. Using different descriptors, Collins (2001) describes the ultimate in leadership as one who gets the right people on the bus (builds a team), the wrong people off the bus, facilitates figuring out the best path to greatness (establishes the aim), and drives the bus (coaches the team).

Climbing the steps to building a team requires self-discipline, personal humility, and professional will. Self-interest and ego take a back seat to the needs of the organization and the team.

IMPLEMENTATION STEPS

1. Agree on the aim

2. Remove organizational practices that damage teamwork

3. Create a consistency of purpose

4. Use data to raise the team's "batting average"

5. Celebrate team successes

6. Champion all-time-bests

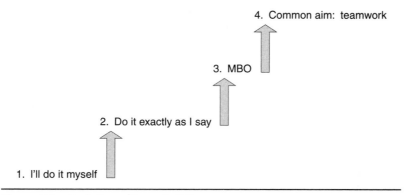

4. Common aim: teamwork

3. MBO

2. Do it exactly as I say

1. I'll do it myself

Figure 2.1 Evolution of team-building.

People want to contribute to a great team and experience the satisfaction of knowing they contributed in a significant manner. However, after years of first-, second-, and third-generation leadership they have gotten the message: *Look out for number one—yourself!* Leaders must determine and analyze the reasons built into the organization for a lack of teamwork. The job of a leader is not to pressure people to cooperate and be a team; this is already built into humans. The job is to remove the system processes (barriers) that derail team-building. Removal will involve sacred cows. The most difficult aspect and most important job in team-building is the second step of implementation: *remove organizational practices that damage teamwork.* Leaders need to hold themselves publicly accountable for barrier removal.

TOOLS

The Force Field Analysis provides a picture of status quo. Organizations experience status quo because the pressure to improve is balanced by just the right amount of resistance. If leaders apply more pressure, others add an equal amount of resistance. The theory behind the Force Field Analysis is that leaders will be more successful removing barriers than adding new reasons for the change. In this instance, we suggest leaders document reasons employees are not working as a team and eliminate them one by one.

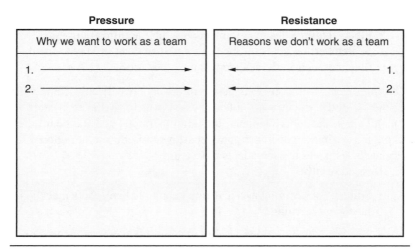

Figure 2.2 Force-field analysis.

EDUCATION EXAMPLES

Common among educators are the beliefs that (1) leaders come and go, (2) the pendulum always swings, and (3) my job is to shut the classroom door and do my best for the kids. Teamwork is nonexistent. In a set of surveys Lee has conducted across several states, educators were asked to describe their organization in terms of four descriptors. The resulting percentages are:

- I work with uncommitted people.   4%

- I work with people doing their best.   40%

- My workplace is a bowling team. We like each   50%
  other, give advice on occasion, and add up scores
  once a year.

- My workplace performs like an orchestra.   6%
  We work together to make beautiful music by
  continually evaluating our performance and
  improving as necessary.

In K–12 education it seems that everything is set up against teamwork:

- Often there are a limited number of A's.

- Educators are told that the ideal would be complete individualization. Every student would have his or her own objective for every
  subject. (Management by objectives is for adults; individualization
  is the same concept for students.)

- States require educators to meet with their administrators in
  September, set goals for the year, and then meet in May to see if
  they met their individualized goals.

The improvement that citizens desire in education will only come when teachers and the students are a team, when principals and their staff are a team, when the superintendent, the administrators, and the board are a team, and when the governor, state department of education, regional service agencies, and superintendents are a team.

Desired results:

- Students performing as a learning team to help teachers meet goals
  in student learning.

- Teachers collaborating to create meaningful curricula focused on
  outcomes of significance for all children.

- Administrators working as a team to passionately drive the process to create the best learning environment possible and remove barriers to success.

- All those connected with the educational community teaming up to improve success and decrease failure by helping kids achieve more.

One final note: many educators are experts at building athletic teams, but are hard pressed to build a learning team. Learning teams, however, are equally possible.

ADDITIONAL EXAMPLES

It is very easy to divide a high school team right down the middle when deciding on scheduling format: traditional six-period day, one of the several block schedules, or trimester. One high school avoided the destructive practice: first, the principal asked the staff to agree on how many days per week they needed to meet with their students. Obviously, they all knew the tug-of-war: the longer the instructional periods, the fewer meetings per week. The staff agreed they could all be happy with four class meetings per week. The job of the principal was then to create a schedule with each teacher meeting with each class four times a week. He did it. He needed a schedule with 24 class meetings. The solution was that Monday through Thursday had five classes while Friday had four classes. People might say, *What a problem! Friday classes have a few more minutes of instruction.* In our opinion this is a minor problem compared to the disgruntlement in so many high schools over the adopted schedule. This example is not meant to be a discourse on scheduling, but an example of team-building through something that is usually so destructive.

An example of another destructive practice, in elementary schools, is general education versus pull-out. One elementary school solved this issue by having all specialists (special education, art, music, PE) teach from 10:00–5:00 instead of 8:00–3:00. General education teachers had their uninterrupted classroom time the first two hours of each day. Some special education students received services through pull-out between 10:00 and 3:00 and some were served after normal school hours; this decision was made in the IEP meeting. Further, the art, music, and PE teachers had from 3:00–5:00 each day to work with groups of students who were particularly gifted in their subject. This schedule creates much more teamwork between specialists and classroom teachers.

Elementary schools often debate the merits of departmentalization. The three fifth-grade teachers have special interests—math, science, and social studies, so they departmentalize. It is hard, however, to make this practice the norm in elementary schools. If the departmentalization occurs in grades 3, 4 and 5, students will have nine different teachers for core subjects over a three-year period. This is a practice most reject even though they know the power of teachers using their strengths with more than one group of students. Another way to look at this dilemma is to create a team of three teachers who share the same students for three years. The team comprises a third-, fourth-, and fifth-grade teacher each with a specialty in math, science, or social studies. Students stay with the team for three years, thus having only three teachers for core subjects in three years. Each teacher teaches their specialty for three grade levels. A look at a possible daily schedule can clarify how this works (Figure 2.3).

In schools that have art, music, and PE specialists, the team could have regularly scheduled team meetings when their students are with one of the three specialists. Again, the importance of working as teams is really the ability to work together to reach the organizational *aim*. Without teamwork, this will not occur consistently. Without teamwork, fewer and fewer all-time-bests are achieved and the culture returns to its previous status.

	Periods 1, 2	Period 3	Period 4	Period 5
3rd—teacher with science expertise	Language arts 3rd grade	3rd science	4th science	5th science
4th—teacher with math expertise	Language arts 4th grade	4th math	5th math	3rd math
5th—teacher with social studies expertise	Language arts 5th grade	5th social studies	3rd social studies	4th social studies

Figure 2.3   Grade 3 through 5 structure.

Core Value

Valuing faculty, staff, and partners by leadership who is not only dependent upon but committed to the knowledge, skills, innovative creativity, and motivation of its workforce.

Baldrige Connection

Describe how your school's work and jobs enable faculty and staff and the organization to achieve high performance. Describe how compensation, career progression, and related workforce practices enable faculty and staff and the school to achieve high performance.

Guiding Questions

How do you organize and manage work and jobs, including skills, to promote cooperation, initiative, empowerment, innovation, and your organizational culture? How do you ensure that the skill levels and experiences of your workforce are equitably distributed (for example, among individual schools or campuses)? How do you organize and manage work and jobs, including skills, to achieve the agility to keep current with educational service needs and to achieve your action plans?

Adapted from *2005 Education Criteria for Performance Excellence.*

RESOURCES AND READING LIST

Blanchard, Ken. 1997. *Gung Ho!: Turn on the People in Any Organization.* New York: William Morrow.

Collins, Jim. 2001. *Good to Great.* New York: HarperCollins.

Cottrell, Vic. "The Hiring Process." Ventures in Excellence.com.

Deming, W. Edwards. January 1992. American Association of School Administrators Conference, Washington, DC.

———. 1994. *The New Economics,* 2nd ed. Cambridge, MA: Massachusetts Institute of Technology Center for Educational Services.

Jenkins, Lee. 2003. *Improving Student Learning: Applying Deming's Quality Principles in Classrooms,* 2nd ed. Milwaukee: ASQ Quality Press.

Roettger, Lloyd O. November 2000. "The Pursuit of Quality in the Academy." Presentation conducted at the fall conference of the Rocky Mountain Educational Research Association, Edmond, OK.

Scholtes, Peter. R. 1998. *The Leader's Handbook: Making Things Happen, Getting Things Done.* New York: McGraw-Hill.

3

Accountability: Staying on Track

OVERVIEW

Accountability means that the team is responsible for meeting the aim. If the aim is to increase success and decrease failure, then the team is accountable for measuring the increases in success and the decreases in failure (Figure 3.1). Accountability is not about evaluating people; it is about the productivity of the team.

Even if a person seemingly works alone, the team is present. A self-employed artist depends on the quality of clay, the foundry, the gallery, the photographer, and the media. Ultimately, the sculptor is most dependent on the joy of customers.

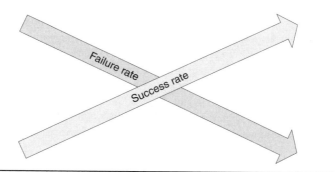

Figure 3.1 The team is accountable for measuring the increases in success and the decreases in failure.

The basic accountability decision that leaders must make is whether to use improvement or arbitrary goals as the measure of success. If last year a car manufacturer, for example, had 2.34 warranty repairs per 100 cars, should factories and engineering teams this year be responsible to simply reduce that number or to reach a goal set by a board of directors? (2.00 warranty repairs per 100 cars, for example)

The difficulty with arbitrary goals is that the automobile company could actually improve significantly and in fact have a better year than ever before—they could have 2.04 warranty repairs per 100 cars—yet the board of directors set the accountability measure at 2.00, so people will suffer the consequences.

IMPLEMENTATION STEPS

The *radar chart* (also called a *spider chart*) is the perfect tool for leaders to visualize multiple measures over multiple years. One way to build it is with Excel. The example in Figure 3.2 shows reading and math results on standardized exams from one school district over an eight-year period.

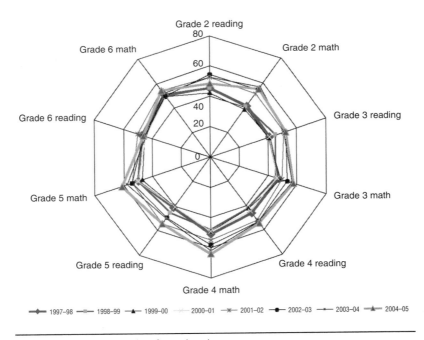

Figure 3.2 An example of a radar chart.

Steps:

A. List accountability measures that are consistent from year to year.

B. Determine success for each measure. This is a value judgment.

C. Calculate percent of students who meet success criteria for each measurement.

D. Enter into a spreadsheet and create radar chart. (Some clean-up may be necessary; wider lines and better colors create a more legible graph.)

E. Look for all-time-bests, which are those points closest to 100 percent successful. Celebrate. (In the example in Figure 3.2, the school district achieved all-time-bests in grades 3, 4, and 5 in math and grades 3, 4, and 5 in reading. Accountability must include data collected over time in a consistent manner. Patterns and trends tell a story that never can be communicated with one or two data points. Collins (2001) asserts that true greatness can be observed in sustained improvement over time (at least seven years). Deming (1994) indicated that multiple metrics collected over the production period best revealed the existence of continuous improvement.

EDUCATION EXAMPLES

Almost all schools have a school improvement document with plans and goals for a myriad of activities from reading to science to graduation rate to discipline and attendance. How does a leader ever communicate to staff, boards, parents, and students whether or not progress was made? The radar chart is an excellent accountability tool.

The suggestion is to put nothing in the school plan that cannot be calculated as a percent successful or percent failing. Assume, for example, that a school includes attendance in its school plan. The next step is to determine what successful attendance is. If a school community agrees on 95 percent, then what percent of students are present 95 percent of the school days (or 95 percent of days after their enrollment)? For the failure radar chart, decide what totally unacceptable attendance is, for example, less than 80 percent. The radar chart is prepared by entering into a spreadsheet program like Excel the successful percent (or failing percent) for each item in the school plan. Year after year of data can be entered and the radar chart will display the line for each year in a different color.

Some school districts have used the required disaggregations from the No Child Left Behind Act of 2001 to create their radar charts to determine what percentage of each subgroup (gender, ethnicity, income level) was successful. Sometimes, state agencies report results with labels such as *not proficient, making progress, proficient,* and *advanced.* The percent of students at *proficient* and *advanced* are used for success and the percent for *not proficient* are used for failing.

Note that in the examples given, there is a certain percentage of students who are not counted as failing or succeeding. There is a purpose in this design. Educators might agree, for example, that students above the 50th percentile are to be counted as successful, but would not count a student at the 49th percentile as failing. However, when educators look at a list of students who scored below the 20th percentile, there is general agreement that the test results are accurate and these students have special needs.

Table 3.1 gives examples of failure and success agreements that schools and school districts might reach.

When the failure web is very difficult to read in that all the data and lines are clustered around the center at zero, this is good. If all the failure levels are near zero, change the scale of the radar chart from 0–100 to 0–5 or so. However, the typical school will have most aspects of their school around zero with a few problems that show up like the proverbial sore thumb, sticking way out from the center and thus very easy to identify.

Table 3.1   Failure and success agreements that schools and school districts might reach.

School aspect	Failure	Success
Attendance	Less than 80 percent	95 percent or higher
Discipline	Three or more referrals	Zero or 1 referral
Writing, on 1 to 4 scale	Level 1	Levels 3 or 4
Second-grade reading fluency	Less than 50 WPM	90 WPM
Graduation	Does not graduate in five years	High school graduation
High school math	Does not pass Algebra I	Pass Algebra I and II, Geometry

---

Core Value

Social responsibility that goes beyond mere compliance.

Baldrige Connection

Summarize your school's key governance, school leadership, and social responsibility results, including evidence of ethical behavior, fiscal accountability, legal compliance, and organizational citizenship. Segment your results by work units, as appropriate. Include appropriate comparative data.

Guiding Questions

What are your key current findings and trends in key measures or indicators of fiscal accountability, both internal and external, as appropriate?

Adapted from *2005 Education Criteria for Performance Excellence.*

RESOURCES AND READING LIST

Collins, Jim. 2001. *Good to Great.* New York: HarperCollins.

Deming, W. Edwards. January 1992. American Association of School Administrators Conference, Washington, DC.

———. 1994. *The New Economics,* 2nd ed. Cambridge, MA: Massachusetts Institute of Technology Center for Educational Services.

Jenkins, Lee. 2003. *Improving Student Learning: Applying Deming's Quality Principles in Classrooms,* 2nd ed. Milwaukee: ASQ Quality Press.

Roettger, Lloyd O. March 2001. "The Baldrige Criteria: A Way to Refocus Educational Leaders." Paper presented at the Professor of Secondary School Administration and Supervision (PSSAS) National Conference, Phoenix, AZ.

Scholtes, Peter R. 1998. *The Leader's Handbook: Making Things Happen, Getting Things Done.* New York: McGraw-Hill.

4

Hiring Well: A Bucket Full of Million-Dollar Decisions

Every superintendent and school board member understands that money must be spent on advice before a million dollar construction project begins. Architects and engineers are not inexpensive and usually their advice is well worth the cost. In fact, school districts are not allowed to build without investing money in their fees.

We are asking the readers now to calculate the cost of an employee over the span of a career. If the employee is with the school system for 25 years at an average cost of $40,000 per year, the employee will earn one million dollars. We are advocating that the million-dollar employee decision is more important than the million-dollar construction decision. Yet administrators often delegate completely the responsibility to hire well. School systems need to invest money in advice on hiring just as they invest money in advice on building.

Establishment of a hiring system is the responsibility of the superintendent. The superintendent may or may not be involved directly in the interviews; this depends on the size of the school district. However, the superintendent must lead the hiring process. When the superintendent leaves a school district, many decisions will be reversed or altered in some way. The personnel hired, however, will embody much of the legacy of the superintendent.

Lee worked with Ventures for Excellence and its president, Dr. Vic Cottrell, while serving as a superintendent. Most of what Lee knows about the employee selection process was gained from Vic, who summarizes 30 years of selection research:

> One of the strengths human beings possess that separates us from all other creatures of this earth is the ability to identify priorities.

These priorities become what we call values. When employing a new person to join our organization, we must acquire an in-depth understanding of their core *values.* In excess of 30 years, Ventures for Excellence associates have studied thousands of people in many different organizations. As a result, we have identified four key values that are absolutely essential for an excellent employee to possess. We find that no employees become excellent unless these four values are clearly evident in their attitudes and behaviors. These values are as follows:

1. *Human worth.* Excellent employees believe in their infinite worth while recognizing that all people they encounter also have infinite worth. They recognize each person with whom they work as an extremely valuable human being and quickly appreciate the unique contributions of their coworkers.

2. *Relationships.* Excellent employees understand and believe in the positive value of relationships with others. As a result, they strive to be good listeners and communicate with others in a manner that creates a mutually supportive and humane environment. These employees possess multiple approaches for building and maintaining excellent relationships with their coworkers.

3. *Human development.* Excellent employees believe they are in a constant process of maximizing their potential. In turn, they believe all coworkers also possess enormous potential for continued growth, learning, and development. In their eyes, all coworkers can learn and will learn. They continuously seek ways to optimize positive learning opportunities for themselves and others. There exists a never-ending thirst for learning and becoming the best they can be.

4. *Practical application.* Excellent employees understand for learning to be effective, immediate application must be made. They are constantly striving to close the gap between *learning* and *doing.* They strive to work with coworkers to make practical applications in new ways of utilizing information and knowledge.

Unless these core values, attitudes, and behaviors are in place, the employees will not be highly effective. In fact, the entire employee environment must create a culture of greatness that centers around these core values. The challenge employers face is to quickly identify these core values as they pragmatically relate to the specific job role of an employee. (Personal letter to authors, January 2006.)

We would describe Vic Cottrell and Stephen Covey as psychologists who study excellence. Most psychologists earn their living studying problems and helping people overcome problems. These two psychologists use similar strengths to study people who are effective. Dr. Cottrell uses the knowledge to help administrators predict future success of job applicants and Dr. Covey uses the knowledge in his writing and speaking.

Not only do personnel offices need to learn how to hire well, they must be accountable for all-time-bests just like everybody else. In personnel, just as in writing, one cannot easily count quality. Educators have used *rubrics* to assist in evaluating student writing for years and the same tool is invaluable for evaluating the effectiveness of personnel. Below is a suggested rubric:

1. This teacher meets the needs of no students or very few students.

2. This teacher meets the needs of half of the students. It is common for some parents and students to praise this teacher and on the same day for other parents and students to complain about this teacher.

3. This teacher meets the needs of all or almost all of the students on a consistent basis. This includes the high-achieving students, as well as the struggling students.

4. This teacher not only meets the needs of all or almost all students, but is a mentor to other teachers on the staff. His/her strengths spread beyond the individual classroom.

Leaders in the school district have the responsibility to (1) document and counsel so that level 1 teachers find their appropriate profession, and (2) provide staff development for level 2 teachers and continue to develop level 3 and 4 teachers. At the end of the year, one aspect of the evaluation of the personnel office is, "Did personnel have an all-time-best? When the rubric scores were all added up, was the total higher than ever before?" Another way to ask about personnel improvement refers back to the success/failure aim: "Do we have fewer level 1 teachers and more level 3 and 4 teachers than ever before?"

We conclude this chapter with directions on hiring grumpy, middle-aged employees. Leaders must know the steps for hiring grumpy, middle-aged employees. It is quite easy to do. The process is to hire young, bubbly, talented, vivacious, selfish employees. In a few years one has grumpy, middle-aged employees. Why? The only choice selfishness has is to turn into bitterness. The bitter employee has a litany of reasons why they are bitter, reasons that involve the faults of others. Here's the problem with their laundry list. Other employees have also been in the same organization for the same period of time. They have had the same bosses, same salary, same union, same coworkers, same regulations, and same budget. Not all are bitter. So the reasons the bitter employees give for their poor attitude do not hold up. If they were true, then why are not all employees bitter?

Selfishness is the reason for the bitterness. Every organization has enough imperfections to give selfish people ample reasons to become bitter. So the responsibility of leaders is to hire unselfish people. Every time a boss laments the hiring of a particular employee, he/she can look back to a time when incredible strength blinded the interview committee to selfishness. The strength, wrapped up in selfishness, has proven to be not worth the cost.

How does one interview for selfishness? Open-ended questions such as, "What is it that gives you the greatest joy in your job?" provide clues. A committee was interviewing architects with this question. All of the candidates, except one, answered the question by describing a building. One candidate said his greatest joy came from returning to the building a year or so after construction and finding happy customers.

Clearly, one question can not determine the extent of selfishness in a candidate, but an organized interview and reference-checking process designed to ascertain selfishness is entirely possible. We urge leaders to spend the time and money to become excellent in hiring. The million-dollar hiring process can be greatly improved.

A caution: Online interviews through the Web can be of great assistance. A well-designed online interview can screen candidates by telling administrators which candidates can describe excellence. However, the online interview can not tell the administrator if the candidate can deliver once hired. This must be done in person.

RESOURCES AND READING LIST

Cottrell, Vic. Ventures for Excellence, 6221 South 58 Street, Suite F, Lincoln, NE 68516. Email: ventures@inebraska.com. Web site: www.venturesfor excellence.com.

Covey, Stephen. 1989. *The 7 Habits of Highly Effective People*. New York: Simon and Schuster.

Welch, Jack, and Suzy Welch. 2006. "So Many CEOs Get This Wrong." *Business Week* (July 17): 92.

5

Results: Are We Improving or Just Changing?

OVERVIEW

Change is a neutral word. Some changes make things worse; some make things better. Improvement is defined as a change that makes an organization or situation better. However, one can not improve unless one changes.

Much has been written about the need to change. Often, the underlying tone indicates that those who refuse to change are somehow inferior to those willing to change. There can be many reasons for a resistance to change. A legitimate reason for resisting a particular change is the belief that the change will make things worse, not better. Most people are interested in improvement and will make the necessary changes that lead to improvement, if they believe it is necessary. However, it is difficult to lead the change process when change after change after change have previously been enacted with no resulting improvement or without sustained professional development.

Educational improvement will not occur until it translates to the classroom. Teachers are the central enactor of all of the administrative-directed answers to reform. Classrooms are the arena for education change (Bascia and Hargraves 2000, Katzenmeyer and Moller 1996, Temes 2002).

"Change is a process, not an event."(Hall and Hord 2006). Gathering baseline data and analyzing the data regularly help teachers see improvement. Without data, during the difficult early innovation stages of change, people can become discouraged. This discouragement can lead to half of the people saying the change improved things and half saying the change made things worse. Whether or not the change survives is a matter of power and personality, not a matter of knowledge. With data driving the change, some of the emotion can be removed and the continuation of the change is much more likely.

CONTINUOUS IMPROVEMENT LEADERSHIP STRATEGIES

1. Develop and nurture a good relationship with teachers and staff.

2. Gather data relentlessly (all data should be analyzed through the lens of improving student achievement).

3. Plan the change using strategic approaches and tactical deployment.

4. Provide training (consistent, aligned professional development).

5. Consistently support the process and the people. (Provide both emotional and material resources, both from leaders and peers.)

6. Review the time available and determine how to provide the necessary time for planning and implementation of the change.

7. Continuously evaluate the data (Roettger 2003). Did the organization experience an all-time-best because of the change?

TOOLS

Dr. Deming gave us the *plan–do–study–act* cycle (Figure 5.1). The essence of the four components is:

Plan. Gather up baseline data, analyze current data, and plan an experiment.

Do. Conduct the experiment.

Study. Study the results of the experiment.

Act. If the experiment resulted in improvement, then act to cement the improvement into the normal processes of the organization. Then start over with a new experiment, always striving to make improvements.

Figure 5.1 PDSA cycle.

It might be helpful in understanding PDSA to examine a common school activity that is the opposite of PDSA—textbook selection.

1. *Plan.* Schools do not know if a new book is needed. They do not know what results were created with the old book and have no way of knowing if the new book will be an improvement.

2. *Do.* Schools have this part mastered; they do adopt a new book.

3. *Study.* No data is collected to see if the new book is an improvement.

4. *Act.* There is no intention of making this adoption stick; it is understood that in seven years this book will go away. All of the hard work to purchase and get used to a new book will be lost to the organization.

It is important that during the planning of the improvement or change process, an agreement is made on the data that will be evaluated and analyzed. A leader may allow a lot of flexibility in the classroom implementation of the process, but agreement on how the staff will know if the change results in improvement should be understood by all. A school or school district that takes the time to agree on how it will know if a change results in improvement is a school or district that is taking one more step to transform the culture into one of expecting all-time-bests.

Core Values

Focus on results and creating value as the means to improving student learning and building loyalty.

Managing for innovation to improve the school and create value for students and stakeholders.

Baldrige Connection

Describe how your school measures, analyzes, aligns, reviews, and improves student and operational performance data and information at all levels and in all parts of your school. How are improvements and lessons learned shared with other organizational units to drive organizational learning and innovation?

Continuous improvement includes ongoing improvements in student learning that may be achieved through such actions as implementing major education initiatives, integrating new technology, refining teaching methods and the curriculum design and development process, or incorporating faculty and staff training and development initiatives.

Guiding Questions

How do you translate organizational performance review findings into priorities for continuous and breakthrough improvement and into opportunities for innovation? How are these priorities and opportunities deployed to faculty and staff throughout your school to enable effective support for their decision making? When appropriate, how are the priorities and opportunities deployed to your feeder and/or receiving schools and to your suppliers and partners to ensure organizational alignment? How do school leaders create an environment for performance improvement, accomplishment of strategic objectives, innovation, and organizational agility? How do they create an environment for organizational and faculty and staff learning?

Adapted from *2005 Education Criteria for Performance Excellence.*

RESOURCES AND READING LIST

Bascia, Nina, and Andy Hargreaves. 2000. *The Sharp Edge of Educational Change.* London: Routledge Falmer.

Chenoweth, Thomas, and Robert Everhart. 2002. *Navigating Comprehensive School Change: A Guide for the Perplexed.* Larchmont, NY: Eye on Education.

Fullan, Michael. 2001. *Leading in a Culture of Change.* San Francisco: Jossey-Bass.

Hall, Gene, and Shirley Hord. 2006. *Implementing Change: Patterns, Principles, and Potholes.* Boston: Allyn & Bacon.

Katzenmeyer, Marilyn, and Gayle Moller. 1996. *Awakening the Sleeping Giant: Leadership Development for Teachers.* Thousand Oaks, CA: Corwin Press.

Roettger, Caroline. 2003. *Change: A Teacher's Perspective.* Unpublished dissertation, Oklahoma State University, Stillwater, OK.

The SEDL Center for Comprehensive School Reform and Improvement Database. http://www.csrclearinghouse.org/index.php?option=com_rdatabase&Itemid=83.

Temes, Peter. 2002. *Against School Reform (And in Praise of Great Teaching.)* Chicago: Ivan R.

6

Responsibility: Management and Leadership

OVERVIEW

Leaders are responsible for both the management and leadership of their organization. As defined by Marcus Buckingham (2005) in *The One Thing You Need to Know, leadership* is meeting the needs all have in common and *management* is meeting the needs unique to individuals. Clearly, both aspects of the organization require leadership. A clear view of management/ leadership is at the core of understanding responsibility.

CONTINUOUS IMPROVEMENT LEADERSHIP STRATEGIES

First, leaders are responsible for meeting the needs of all. Everyone needs the plane to land safely, everyone needs safe drinking water, everyone needs clean air to breathe, and all students need to enjoy learning in school. However, since there is no such thing as a perfect organization, there is room for improvement. Leaders are responsible to (1) document gaps, (2) lead people in improvement efforts, and (3) document which efforts were successful and unsuccessful.

Leaders in education have different names: governor, superintendent, principal, and teacher. Each has a group of people for whom they are responsible. Yes, they may have assistance, but the responsibility for meeting the needs of all belongs to the leader and cannot be delegated.

Leaders delegate management responsibilities as often as possible. Management is meeting the unique needs of individuals. In a school system, bus drivers have certain needs versus the needs of cooks. While kindergarten and 12th-grade teachers have more in common than not, there are unique needs for various grade levels and subjects. Leaders must both meet these needs and provide a mechanism for feedback for the delegated tasks.

TOOL FOR REPORTING ON DELEGATED TASKS

Leaders, when assigning tasks, should also assign reporting timelines. An example of a reporting hierarchy is below:

1. Report in person each week.

2. Report via e-mail each week.

3. Report in person once each month.

4. Report via e-mail each month.

5. Report in person once each quarter.

6. Report via e-mail each quarter.

Such a reporting system assists the leader with their management responsibilities. It is not a "go forth and hope for the best" strategy, but a system of specific responsibilities with a reporting structure. The employees like knowing how and when they are to report progress on assigned duties. They want to be responsible, and the leader sets up the scaffolding that enables them.

IMPLEMENTATION STEPS

It is easy to become so involved in management tasks that there remains little time for leadership responsibilities. Step one is to list leadership jobs. What do all the people for whom I am responsible need? The next step is to allocate time each week to meet such responsibilities. Stephen Covey's four quadrants of time management, described in *The 7 Habits of Highly Effective People,* provide a means of classifying management and leadership responsibilities. We would encourage readers to revisit Chapter 3 of Covey's book. Covey (2004) classifies tasks as *important/not important* and *urgent/not urgent* (Table 6.1).

We inserted the words *management* and *leadership* into Covey's matrix. His book lists examples of activities in each quadrant. When we compared Buckingham's distinction between management and leadership

Table 6.1 Covey's management and leadership responsibilities.

	Urgent	Not urgent
Important	I. Management	II. Leadership
Not important	III. Management	IV. Management

with Covey's admonishment to work in quadrant II as much as possible, we saw leadership fitting into quadrant II. Covey wrote, "You have to decide what your highest priorities are and have the courage—pleasantly, smilingly, nonapologetically—to say 'no' to other things." There will never be enough time to complete 100 percent of the management tasks. "The key is not to prioritize what's on your schedule, but to schedule your priorities," continues Covey. We would say that if you do not schedule the time when you are meeting needs that all have in common, it will not occur.

FURTHER EXAMPLES

Lee was in a large, urban middle school with three assistant principals. Each was spending 100 percent of their time on student discipline. He suggested that the assistant principals each set aside two hours a week when they would receive no discipline referrals. The other two APs would cover for them. During these two hours they were to work on improving the discipline system, which in time would reduce the number of referrals. Lee saw these two hours as leadership time. The suggestion was rejected because there was no time—too many referrals. From our perspective, leaders must practice leadership at least some of the time, and clearly these three assistant principals did not see themselves as leaders, but as clerks dealing with whatever somebody else thought was important.

Core Values

Management by fact that uses performance measurement to focus on improving student learning.

Social responsibility. A school's leaders should stress responsibilities to the public, ethical behavior, and the need to practice good citizenship. Leaders should be role models for your school in focusing on ethics and protection of public health, safety, and the environment.

Continued

Continued

Baldrige Connection

Continuous improvement includes implementing major education initiatives, integrating new technology, refining teaching methods and the curriculum design and development process, or incorporating faculty and staff training and development initiatives. Describe how your school measures, aligns, reviews, analyzes, and improves student performance data and information at all levels and in all parts of your school. How are improvements and lessons learned shared with other organizational units to drive organizational learning and innovations?

Guiding Questions

What are your results for key measures or indicators of accomplishment of your organizational strategy and action plans? What are your results for key measures or indicators of ethical behavior and of stakeholder trust in the school leaders and governance of your school? What are your results for key measures or indicators of breaches of ethical behavior? What are your key current findings and trends in key measures or indicators of fiscal accountability, both internal and external, as appropriate? What are your results for key measures or indicators of regulatory, safety, accreditation, and legal compliance? What are your results for key measures or indicators of organizational citizenship in support of your key communities?

Adapted from *2005 Education Criteria for Performance Excellence.*

RESOURCES AND READING LIST

Buckingham, Marcus. 2005. *The One Thing You Need to Know.* New York: The Free Press.

Covey, Stephen. 1989. *The 7 Habits of Highly Effective People.* New York: Simon and Schuster.

7

Communication: It's More Than Words

OVERVIEW

When one *Googles* "communication and leadership," over 77,700,000 results are returned. Obviously, a critical relationship exists between the two. In fact, the importance of effective communication to leaders is demonstrated daily in all organizations. School leaders have the responsibility of establishing strong lines of communication with teachers and among students. Effective communication skills are critical to the success of implementing continuous improvement processes in schools. One could conclude that principals and other school leaders must place the highest value on effective interpersonal communication because they know that increasing teacher productivity and student achievement depends on effective communication. Indeed, various studies (Barnett 2006, Spinks and Wells 1995) have concluded that communication was the main task of managers, leaders, and executives, and that emphasis has been placed on improving communication in most, if not all, organizations. The role of communication in education was one of a small number of issues at the forefront as the practice of continuous improvement emerged from its origins in Deming's work in quality.

Principals and school leaders must keep parents, teachers, students, and staff informed. However, not only is communication from the top important; members of the school community need to keep each other and their leaders informed. In other words, to be effective, communication channels need to be open throughout the organization. The primary responsibility for communication in schools rests with those in leadership positions since everyone else take cues on how to communicate from those in leadership positions. What, then, can a leader do to improve communication in his or her school(s)?

IMPLEMENTATION STEPS

Provide a Good Working Environment

The first step in improving communication is to provide a good working climate. Educators, in large measure, are the kind of communicator that the organization motivates them to be. One of the most compelling factors influencing communication is the organizational climate imposed by the leaders. For example, a flexible climate that can adapt to the complex and changing nature of individual and school needs is one that encourages shared responsibility for continuously improving the learning environment.

The principal or school leader that establishes such a climate can anticipate that feelings of self-worth and respect for others likely will increase throughout the system. Establishment of the appropriate organizational climate promotes effective communication.

There are positive steps a leader can take to improve communication in the school. Often leaders shy away from simple lists of suggestions and guidelines. Yet by following basic suggestions, administrators can become better leaders and enhance communication. Here then are practical suggestions for effective communication.

Encourage Feedback

Start by encouraging feedback. Students can and should be providing teachers feedback about the classes they are taking. Teachers can and should be providing principals feedback about the leadership they are providing. Principals can and should be providing senior leaders feedback about the decisions they are making. Finally, the administrative team should be giving feedback to the school board about the policies they are establishing.

Tell teachers you want feedback. Encourage them to give you both good and bad news. Welcome disagreement on issues. Then, make certain you positively reinforce rather than punish them for such information. Next, listen and encourage feedback rather than taking issue with comments raised by others. Watch for nonverbal cues. Most persons do not control nonverbal responses as well as verbal ones. Some people communicate more by actions than by words. Consider scheduling feedback sessions; a planned feedback session will usually get more response than the passing question, "How are things going?" Use structuring comments to encourage feedback. Statements such as "Tell me more about it," or "That's interesting," help encourage discussion. Ask questions rather than always answering questions. Start your questions with *What, Why, When, Where,* and *How* to encourage feedback.

Listen for Understanding

Learn to listen; it is the most neglected communication skill. All leaders have had instruction in reading, writing, and speaking. Few, however have had any formal instruction in listening. This lack of instruction is especially interesting in light of research showing that people spend seven out of every 10 minutes awake in some form of communication: 10 percent writing, 15 percent reading, 30 percent talking, and 45 percent listening. (Steil and Bommelie 2004)

Here are some things you can do to improve your listening skills. First, realize that effective listening requires preparation. Put away anything that may take your attention away from the speaker such as papers and books. Do not try to multitask during a conversation. Move out from behind your desk to a neutral location if possible. Put your phone on hold so that a call does not interfere with the discussion. Avoid unnecessary interruptions. Lloyd used to tell his secretary not to interrupt him unless the building was on fire. (That only happened once, when some students poured lighter fluid on the plastic toilet seats and lit them.) Be ready to catch the speaker's opening remarks. The rest of the message often builds on the opening statement. Listen for ideas, not just for facts. Keep an open mind. Do not allow yourself to daydream; thought operates several times faster than the normal rate of speech, so use this time differential to summarize and internalize the message. Finally, put yourself in the speaker's place and try to understand the speaker's perspective. Ask questions to clarify and repeat what the speaker says as a means for checking for understanding.

Have a Process to Reach Consensus

One of the biggest problems principals and other school leaders face is getting a group to reach consensus. There are many times, of course, when you must make an independent decision and stick to it. However, shared decision making increasingly is necessary. In the tools section of this chapter we have included a consensus-building process. The basic steps are (1) clarify the discussion, (2) use process statements, (3) seek different views, (4) remain open to different views, and (5) use group pronouns.

The school system is improved when the teachers and administrators work together to improve their teaching abilities, which in turn will result in higher student achievement. When administrators involve the other system members in the decision-making process, schoolwide ownership of reform is more likely to occur.

TOOLS

Continuous Improvement Communication Procedures

Internal

- Principals and other school leaders should restructure staff meetings to focus on operational issues and lessons learned
- Instructional staff should plan meetings every two weeks; regular updates via e-mail and Web site
- Department chairs and team leaders should plan daily meetings with their team and regular meetings with their department

Leaders

- Superintendent and other school leaders should have weekly meetings to report progress

External

- Principals from other schools should meet to discuss transformation, welcome their insights and assistance, plan to update monthly
- Community stakeholders—monthly updates
- Union leadership—monthly updates
- School improvement team—monthly updates

Cooperative Processing

Cooperative processing is a process that Lloyd uses to promote effective communication. He learned this process almost 20 years ago while working in central Iowa as a curriculum director but cannot find or remember the source. There are four key elements of the process: *response, clarification, discussion,* and *decision*. Divide into groups of four. Assign roles to the members of the group: *leader, recorder, reporter,* and *encourager*. The roles of the leader and the recorder are:

Leader

1. Start session
2. Monitor process
3. Make sure everyone has an opportunity to speak
4. Make sure everyone speaks in turn
5. Make sure only one person at a time is speaking

Recorder

1. Record statements
2. Do not edit
3. Number each item

Everyone participates in brainstorming the solution. The important elements of formal brainstorming are:

- Equal opportunity to participate
- Everyone speaks in turn
- Every contribution accepted
- Recorder captures all statements verbatim
- No one can dominate
- No discussion is allowed in this phase and no disagreement, all ideas are valued
- Efficient means of gathering information
- Efficient means of soliciting opinions

Next is the *clarification* component:

- Examine items for clear understanding.
- Explanations given by the person who contributed the item.
- Clarify only. No discussion!
- Use in-turn response and pass rule.

The *discussion* component is the next element. Each participant has the opportunity to offer pro/con statements.

Pro:

- Speak on behalf of any item on the list
- No debate
- Do not repeat opinions already stated

Con:

- Speak on behalf of eliminating an item
- No debate
- Do not repeat opinions already stated

Next, the group participates in the *decision/voting* components. First is a simple clear-out voting activity:

- Majority rule
- Consider each item
- Vote open-hand for *yes,* closed-hand for *no*
- Everyone must vote on each item
- *You cannot pass*
- If majority votes no on an item, it is removed from the list

The final element is weighted voting:

- Vote by assigning value to each item.
- Highest rating is group selection.
- Conduct final vote by *yes/no,* if necessary.
- Vote on each item. *You cannot pass.*

In summary, cooperative processing does the following:

- Provides equal opportunities for contributing ideas
- Forces participation
- Prevents domination
- Keeps group focused at all times
- Achieves higher degree of efficiency
- Promotes better communication

Plus/Delta

Another communication tool is known as a *plus/delta* chart. Plus/delta is one of the simplest of tools to assist communication. At regular intervals, the teachers provide one to the students, and the administrators provide one to the staff. On the plus side, people are to write what went well since the last plus/delta, and on the delta side, they are to write suggestions for making the future better.

Next, the ideas are gathered up and recorded on one sheet of paper (see Figure 7.1). It is imperative that the leader not give the impression that every suggestion can be implemented. People generally seem happy if they know their leader makes at least one change each time a plus/delta is administered.

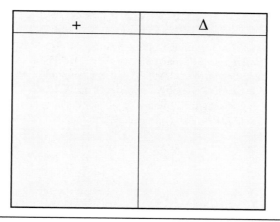

Figure 7.1 Plus/delta chart.

Core Value

Organizational and personal learning that is directed not only toward better educational programs and services, but also toward being more flexible, adaptive, and responsive to the needs of students and stakeholders.

Baldrige Connection

Describe how school leaders guide and sustain your school. Describe how school leaders communicate with faculty and staff and encourage high performance.

Continued

Continued

Guiding Questions

How do school leaders communicate with, empower, and motivate all faculty and staff throughout the school? How do school leaders encourage frank, two-way communication throughout the school? How do senior leaders take an active role in faculty and staff reward and recognition to reinforce high performance and a focus on the school, as well as on students and stakeholders?

Adapted from *2005 Education Criteria for Performance Excellence.*

RESOURCES AND READING LIST

Barnett, Debroah J. 2006. "Strong Communications Skills a Must for Today's Leaders." *Handbook of Business Strategy* 7, no. 1: 385–98.

Spinks, Nelda, and Barron Wells. 1995. "Quality Communication Is a Key to Quality Leadership." *Training for Industry* 3, no. 2: 14–19.

Steil, Lyman K., and Richard K. Bommelie. 2004. *Listening Leaders: The Ten Golden Rules to Listen, Lead and Succeed.* Edina, MN: Beavers Pond Press.

8

Relationships:
The 1:1 Factor

OVERVIEW

In a 1977 seminar Peter Drucker was addressing an audience of 200 bosses. He asked, "How many of you are having a significant problem with one of your employees?" Few hands were raised. Then he asked, "How many of you are having a significant problem with your boss?" Most hands were raised.

Administrator relations is a significant factor in the lives of leaders. In many respects it determines whether or not the leader is able to continue helping people. People seem to have ranked the order in which they will meet the needs of others. Perhaps they rank people above them in the organization first, then people below them, and finally people equal to them. Think about the people you work with. Which of them rank this way—people above, people equal, people below—and which rank people below, people above, people equal. There will also be some who rank people equal as number one.

People want to work for an administrator that ranks the people who report to him/her at the top of the list. We all want to know that the administrator cares for us and we are their top concern. However, if leaders do not take care of the administrator's needs, the leader will move on and be unable to meet the needs of the staff. This chapter is about how to meet the needs of employees and customers as number one and still carry out the responsibilities demanded by the administrator.

Crucial to working with this dilemma is the fact that the administrator may be stupid, inconsiderate, and generally not fun to be around. However, the administrator almost always has more information than the subordinate.

Many things will not make sense to the subordinate. They could make sense if the administrator could share all he/she knows, but this cannot be done. So some aspects of administrator relationships won't make sense.

Another complicating factor with administrator relations is that the more promotions one receives, the more bosses. School superintendents generally have five—bosses elected to a school board.

From 100 interviews with school administrators Vic Cottrell synthesized the strengths, in regard to relationships, of great leaders. He wrote, "This educational leader desires to acquire and maintain trusting and positive relationships with others. This person openly expresses thoughts and feelings while encouraging others to do likewise. There is an ability to have extended and enduring relationships based upon trust and mutual respect for others as valuable human beings."

He also listed apparent weaknesses from these interviews. The percentage next to the statement is the percent out of the 100 interviewees who could describe specific ways to communicate:

- Describe specific ways to build and maintain   23%
  excellent relationships with students

- Describe specific effective ways of building good   17%
  relationships with employees when under criticism

- Describe specific on-going ways of building and   27%
  maintaining good relationships with parents

- Describe specific techniques of observation or   8%
  communication to increase employee effectiveness

- Describe specific ways of facilitating on-going   20%
  effective employee communication with each other

- Describe specific ways of seeking parental views   28%
  using on-going personalized techniques

- Describe specific ways of building and maintaining   23%
  good communication and relationships with
  media personnel

- Describe specific ways to understand the feelings   21%
  of employees in terms of employees "here and
  now" experiences

The 1:1 factor is a key piece of advice from Dr. Cottrell. Suppose you have 20 minutes to talk with your staff. Is it better to have one meeting with four people or better to have four five-minute 1:1 conversations? Dr. Cottrell clearly recommends the four 1:1 conversations as the better way to develop positive relationships.

RESOURCES AND READING LIST

Cottrell, Vic. "Qualities of an Excellent Superintendent." *Ventures for Excellence* information brochure, Lincoln, NE.

Covey, Stephen R. 2004. *The 8th Habit.* New York: Simon and Schuster.

———. 1989. *The 7 Habits of Highly Effective People.* New York: Simon and Schuster.

9

Curriculum and Instruction: The "L" and the "J"

OVERVIEW

In the simplest of terms, *curriculum* is what students are to learn and *instruction* is how teachers are going to teach them this content. When schools are successful with both responsibilities, the students do not know the content of the new course at the onset of the course. When the results of a pretest are graphed, they should be in the shape of an "L" on a histogram. Likewise, when instruction works, the posttest graphed results will be in the shape of a "J" on a histogram. The infamous bell-shaped curve is appropriate for the middle of the school year. The desired results occur when curriculum is appropriate for the grade level and instruction is appropriate for the students. The matrix displayed in Figure 9.1 shows the possible intersection of curriculum and instruction.

Education does not often have this perfect "L to J" but leaders must know what is ideal. They need to know that when the pretest results are already a bell-shaped curve that the curriculum is not rigorous enough and when the posttest results are bell-shaped, the instructional strategies did not work well enough.

This sounds simple but it requires seeing school improvement with a wide lens. The wide-lens view reveals four critical factors: the importance of teacher-developed, aligned curriculum, the power of improving classroom instruction via implementation of continuous improvement, the importance of using data to make good decisions, and the role that assessment plays in encouraging learners toward continuous improvement.

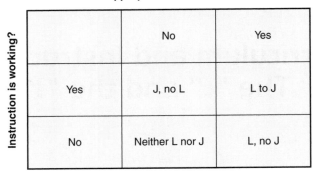

Figure 9.1   The L to J matrix for curriculum and instruction.

EDUCATION EXAMPLE

Perhaps the best way to illustrate these critical factors is to relate the success story of Miami, Arizona. Like a lot of at-risk, failing districts, Miami had limited resources. However, they knew that the curriculum was failing their students, so they began with an attempt to rewrite the curriculum from a K–12 point of view. The initial efforts failed because the process was labor-intensive, not teacher-friendly, and did not provide an easily monitored data-gathering process for student assessment. They needed a system that focused efforts on improving learning for the students while growing and developing the staff. They also quickly realized that to lead and sustain the improvement effort they needed someone who could relate to the teachers, conduct the training effectively, and commit to sustained follow-up over the course of the journey to excellence. Continuous, focused professional development and support are essential to the improvement process. First, a basic philosophy was established by agreeing on eight elements that would be essential to the success of the project. These eight essential elements of the successful continuous improvement journey include:

- Improvement must focus on creating more success and less failure in learning for students

- For improvement to happen, adults must grow and develop

- For improvement to happen, the fear of failure must be removed

- To improve test scores, you must improve the instructional process

- To improve the instructional process, you must improve the curriculum

- Test scores are not the end; helping students learn to think using the skills they develop is the end

- Developing aligned curriculum and assessments are essential for achieving improvement

- Committed administrative support in the form of instructional leadership is necessary (Roettger and Roettger 2005)

Jenkins (2003) provided the principles for improving the instructional process through assessment, and Roettger and Roettger provided the process for improving the curriculum through aligning teacher-developed curriculum to state standards and high-stakes tests, customized to local district needs.

The project was a three-year process. The goals for the school improvement project were to implement the L to J process, develop quality curriculum, create classroom assessments, use quality tools and Teacher Expectations for Student Achievement (TESA) to improve instruction, use effective-schools research to improve administration and operations, increase student success, and decrease student failure. As a result, the school district began a journey of continuous improvement. The first step was a four-day workshop with the aim of training the administrators to lead the process. Following the administrator preparation, initial training started with a pilot group of interested teachers participating in a four-day summer workshop with the aim of spreading the word to other staff. After this training, an additional week was spent developing curriculum for use in the upcoming school year. Wiggins (2004) refers to this as designing for understanding. Over the ensuing three-month period, nearly 95 percent of the district's staff attended one of the initial workshops during the monthly staff development day. First was the implementation of curriculum development K–8, which resulted in unit designs and lesson assessment of essential learnings for math, reading, writing, and language arts. The high school improvement efforts began with TESA training and effective-schools research dissemination; both are actively being implemented.

The creation of student-centered, continuous improvement curriculum development resulted in a series of teaching units with aligned objectives, essential learning facts, teaching and learning ideas, assessment strategies, celebrated educational experiences, teacher guide pages, a scope and sequence, a culminating experience to demonstrate deeper understanding, and a student mastery profile. The curriculum development process includes the following steps:

1. Establishing graduation goals

2. Reviewing the state curriculum standards to decide which goals the standards best support

3. Selecting the most important concepts to be taught

4. Developing comprehensive teaching units for each concept

5. Identifying the desired outcomes of the unit:

   a. Determine the culminating activity to demonstrate learning (a celebratable experience).

   b. Select significant performance objectives (the essential components of knowledge, competence, and orientations that are needed to enable the learner to successfully produce the culminating activity).

   c. Decide the enabling objectives for the unit. (The building blocks that provide the basic and essential skills students will need to produce performance and culminating objectives. This is the *vocabulary* for deeper understanding.)

6. Identifying the essential facts learners need to know

7. Creating assessments of those facts

8. Determining mastery criteria

9. Designing lessons that deliver aligned instruction

The majority of the K–8 teachers almost immediately saw the merits of continuous improvement and began implementation coached by their trained peers and led and supported by their administrators. The simplicity of the system used in this continuous improvement effort made sense to the teachers and provided a new hope for success.

The results were amazing and real. Before the beginning of the project, all four buildings in the district were falling far below standards and were considered low-performing. None had ever made adequate yearly progress (AYP). The 2005 round of standardized testing resulted in all four buildings meeting AYP and all four being rated as performing, performing plus, or excellent! The lower elementary was the only school in the state that went from "falling far below" standard to "excellent" in one year. The junior high reported that 94 percent of its students are now making A's, B's, or C's, a dramatic improvement, accompanied by high standards and more difficult curriculum. Absenteeism has been reduced for both students and teachers districtwide.

The preceding case study is included to assist leaders with improving both curriculum and instruction. The invisible, hard work is getting the curriculum right so that the pretest results are an "L." Our observations are that about half of the time the pretest results show a bell shape; the curriculum is too easy. The body of the case study is about the instruction. What did the Miami, Arizona, staff do the create the "J's?" This is the visible, very hard work. When the curriculum is right, as shown by the L-shaped graph, and the instruction is right, as shown on the J-shaped graph, the test scores will be right. Again, test scores are not the *aim,* improved student learning is the *aim.*

Figure 9.2 shows Mrs. Lanphar's 7th-grade language arts class in Miami, Arizona, in the upper right-hand quadrant as an example of curriculum just right for the grade level and instructional practices that met the students' needs. The other three histogram pairs display either need for instructional improvement, curriculum improvement, or both.

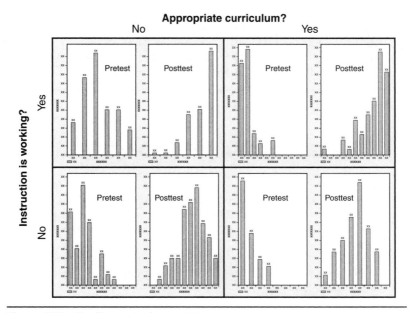

Figure 9.2   Quality curriculum matrix.

Core Values

Learning-centered education that places the focus of education on learning and the real needs of students.

Focus on results and creating value as the means to improving student learning and building loyalty.

Baldrige Connection

Examples include the effectiveness of curriculum and instruction, assessment of student learning, participation in professional development opportunities, and student placement following program completion. Continuous improvement includes ongoing improvements for student learning that may be achieved through such actions as implementing major education initiatives, integrating new technology, refining teaching methods and the curriculum design and development process, or incorporating faculty and staff training and development initiatives.

Guiding Questions

What critical content must be taught to achieve the desired educational outcomes? How can the curriculum best be deployed to ensure that students have the background knowledge, the requisite skills, and the essential facts necessary to achieve academically at high standards? What classroom assessment practices best provide for increased intrinsic motivation of the learners? What quality tools are most likely to produce results that will improve the metrics of student achievement? What culminating experience can help the student utilize the information to develop a deeper understanding or meaning?

Adapted from *2005 Education Criteria for Performance Excellence.*

RESOURCES AND READING LIST

Jenkins, Lee. 2003. *Improving Student Learning: Applying Deming's Quality Principles In Classrooms,* 2nd ed. Milwaukee: ASQ Quality Press.

McTighe, Jay, and Grant Wiggins. 2004. *Understanding by Design: Professional Development Workbook*. Alexandria, VA: Association for Supervision and Curriculum Development.

Roettger, Lloyd, and Caroline Roettger. 2005. "Making Curriculum Sense Out of the Standards Movement." Paper presented at the International Conference on Education. Honolulu, HI.

10

Critical Success Factors: Putting it All Together

OVERVIEW

Public education generally has only 13 years to accomplish its mission. A few students take 14 years, and some finish in 12 years or less, but the norm is 13 years. What does society want from its schools? What is success? There are a lot of different demands, but what are the critical success factors?

For the authors, the critical success factors are enthusiasm and learning. When schools are successful, the students still love learning in school and they are prepared for the next level of education or the workforce. What does this mean in reality?

It means that at the end of elementary school, the students go onto middle school as excited about learning in school as they were when they entered kindergarten and they have the skills and knowledge necessary to succeed in middle school. It means that at the end of middle school, the students go on to high school as excited about learning in school as they were when they entered middle school and they have the skills and knowledge necessary to succeed in high school. It means that at the end of high school, the students go on to higher education, the military, or the general workforce as excited about learning as they were when they entered high school and have the skills and knowledge necessary to succeed in post-K–12 life.

The basic understanding is that students enter kindergarten with all the enthusiasm they will need for life but have little knowledge or skills necessary for post-K–12 life. So one set of success factors is not about growth, but about maintaining entry-level attitudes. The other set of success factors is about gain.

It is the responsibility of each school district to measure the critical success factors at the end of each level of education and note the percent of attainment. Each individual school is to design its school plan around closing the gap between perfect scores on success factors and the reality of today. Are this year's graduates the best prepared ever?

Let's First Manage What We Can Measure

This axiom, while intuitive for most managers and business professionals, is often not applied to education by school leaders. While there are tremendous differences in management styles and priorities from district to district, one thing is clear: the principals that focus on continuously measuring their personal management/leadership behaviors, including aligning initiatives and priorities, create and lead more effective schools than those who leave it to chance.

Other principals who do not attend to critical success factors have experienced a lesser degree of success and organizational buy-in by their teachers and staff. Review of these failures and shortfalls has generally concluded that the lack of attention to the critical success factors, for a sustained period, creates a leadership vacuum around the principal's school improvement program. Without this attention to critical success factors, the reactive culture returns and overcomes the school improvement initiative. Human nature dictates that most revert to the old way, the comfortable way of doing things, when under stress.

Positive results do not come easily and require many factors besides leadership alignment. Without the statistics, the charts, the projects, and the training, desired results can not be realized. Equally, the lack of alignment between people and school improvement strategies can quickly derail the best-intentioned school improvement initiative. This can quickly divert the attention of the principal. Every day there are opportunities to either focus on the essential or to lose focus and react to incidental crises. What must be done and which decisions deserve priority treatment are among the hundreds of choices principals make daily. A principal must be equipped to make the right choices. In other words, what is most important, most essential, or most critical needs to get done.

Critical Success Factors and Focus

During most administrator preparation programs some discussion of the critical success factors takes place. These discussions vary greatly in depth of coverage but usually include a variety of content including instructional leadership, teacher empowerment, parent involvement, communications, resources, projects, discipline, and more.

Each one of these critical success factors contributes to building a culture of all-time-bests and may be broken down into subfactors to further define the actions, measurements, roles, responsibilities, and behaviors that the school must demonstrate to assure success and get significant results. An examination of a few critical success factors and their associated subfactors is provided for more clarification. Critical success factors are those things that must be in place for the school to achieve its aim.

We have adapted the following material for education from *Six Sigma Critical Success Factors* by Bruce J. Hayes.

Critical Success Factors for Instructional Leadership

- You must work at maintaining an active role in communication.

- You must consistently support your teachers and staff.

- You must be accessible and visible in your building(s). (Brenda Emanuel, Sheldon, Texas, principal, often takes her laptop and a stack of paperwork into the back of classrooms to complete assigned duties and know what is happening in school. She credits "Breakthrough Coach" staff development for this concept.)

- You must give specific recognition for successes.

- Consistently foster linkage of instruction to school improvement strategies.

- Make evident and clear your prioritization of initiatives, programs, and priorities.

- Always require data and the use of facts to support actions at all levels of decision making.

- Firmly establish accountabilities, expectations, roles, and responsibilities for all personnel under the principal's direction.

- Conduct and attend to regular teacher performance evaluations to assure and verify continuous improvement.

- Always practice being N.E.A.T.: provide *notice, explanation, assistance,* and *time.*

Critical Success Factors for Communications

- Communicate regularly with teachers to develop positive relationships and learn of all-time-bests

- Create and communicate a plan to support the teachers in their roles

- Regularly provide written communications on school news and successes

- Provide professional development and dissemination of communication aids to the staff

- Create, advocate, and use a common vocabulary based on continuous quality improvement

- Communicate pertinent facts in every faculty meeting, avoid gripe sessions, and foster learning sessions

Critical Success Factors for Programs and Projects

- Document and inventory all the programs, projects, grants, and so on, in the school or system

- Assure linkage of programs and projects to critical school and student needs

- Establish programs and projects of achievable scope and size

- Assign an administrator/leader and teacher to each program or project and hold them accountable

- Implement a follow-up system to facilitate efficiency

- Allow enough time for success

When setting standards you get what you expect. High expectations in standards often improve results (and the reverse is true).

Develop critical success factors with a stakeholders committee using external and internal scanning. The stakeholders can also suggest possible metrics/measures of the critical success factors. Some examples include:

- Progress of students on basic skills

- Passing rates on graduation examinations

- Employment status of graduates

- Performance of transfer students

- Passing rates of students in developmental courses

- Success rate of special education students in mastering grade-level standards

- Satisfaction of program completers and noncompleters

- Curriculum-specific program student retention and graduation

- Employer satisfaction with graduates

- Program unduplicated head count enrollment

The Power of Alignment

Reviewing this book in manuscript form prompted ASQ member James B. Kohnen, a retired colonel from the U.S. Army, to note the following: "A good friend and author George Labovitz introduced me to the concept of organizational alignment several years ago. In his book *The Power of Alignment*, he presents a compelling case for the need for organizational alignment and highlights 30 years of research connecting alignment to success. The basis of his alignment concept is to collect a large sample of data from the various layers of an organization based on a series of factors and subfactors. The data is objective in that instead of asking people how they think they are doing with their own work, you ask employees and management how the organization is doing with its work regarding a set of specific statements. The data are referenced to a quantitative scale (0–7 for example) and the subfactors are defined in such a way that the responses may be 'drilled,' demographically sorted, summarized, and analyzed. When these data are statistically analyzed and displayed, many strengths, weaknesses, and gaps can be visually identified. Because George was a fighter pilot for the United States Air Force he likes to look at things using the analogy of a 'target.' Applying this to management alignment, his preferred display was one that plotted a 'numerical gap analysis' on a radar type of chart. The closer that the scores are toward the middle of the target, the tighter the alignment and the higher the probability of success. The United States Navy and Federal Express, to mention a couple of organizations, have used this concept successfully."

TOOL

Strategy Map

With the proliferation of Web-based tools, measuring, leading, managing, and improving with data have become easier and much more efficient. If your school has a need to improve, measuring critical success factors and using them to drive optimization is key to your success. See Figure 10.1.

For leaders, whether in the classroom or in administration, it is important to have all students and staff complete a strategy map. Then a composite strategy map can be created, shared with all of the students or staff, and utilized for future action.

	Are decisions made in concert with aim?	Are we working as an orchestra?	Do we have a culture of all-time-bests?	Is the hiring system well defined to provide better and better employees?	Are changes resulting in improvement?	Do we set aside time for Quadrant II, leadership planning/tasks?	Do people listen to their students and employees?	Do we have both an "L" and a "J" in most subjects?	Are relationships among students and staff positive?
Always									
Usually									
50/50									
Rarely									
Never									

Figure 10.1 Strategy map.

FURTHER EXAMPLES

Our reason for including Baldrige criteria in each chapter is to assist readers in their focus on critical success factors. Baldridge is about batting 1.000; it will assist the leader in determining what critical success factors are necessary for perfection. No organization is perfect, but with the assistance of Baldrige criteria every organization can raise its batting average. See Table 10.1 for an example of potential critical success factors in education.

Table 10.1   Examples of potential critical success factors.

Critical success factor	Source of CSF	Primary measures and targets
Increase number of students	Community	Student retention rate
Install PC-based student service— homework hot line	Strategy	Student queries answered in one hour during after-school hours (5:00 to 9:00 PM)
Increase number of student A's with raised academic expectations—not grade inflation	Strategy	Number of A's per 100 students
Decrease class size	Strategy	Reduce class-size variation
Raise teacher morale and productivity	Temporal	Increase teacher retention rate
Increase principal effectiveness rating	NASSP/NAESP	Improve rating

---

Core Values

Focus on results and creating value as the means to improving student learning and building loyalty.

Focus on the future that takes into account both short-term and longer-term factors that affect the school.

Management by fact that uses performance measurement to focus on improving student learning.

Continued

Continued

Baldrige Connection

Describe your school's key processes for gaining knowledge about your current and future students, stakeholders, and markets, with the aim of offering relevant and effective programs and services, understanding emerging student and stakeholder requirements and expectations, and keeping pace with market changes and changing methods of delivering educational services.

Determine what factors are critical for your operations and implement systematic processes for sharing this information.

Measurement, analysis, and knowledge management serve as a foundation for the performance management system and are critical to the effective management of your school and to a fact-based, knowledge-driven system for improving performance.

Guiding Questions

What critical incidents, such as complaints, can be utilized to understand critical education and support service attributes from the point of view of students, stakeholders, faculty, and staff.

Schools have a critical need to provide an effective analytical basis for decisions because resources for improvement are limited and cause–effect connections often are unclear.

Adapted from *2005 Education Criteria for Performance Excellence.*

RESOURCES AND READING LIST

Green, Carlton. 2005. *What is the Purpose of a Banana? Critical Success Factors for Effective Leadership.* Fresno, CA: Lessismoore Publishing.

Hayes, Bruce. n.d. "Six Sigma Critical Success Factors." iSixSigma Retrieved from http://www.isixsigma.com/library/content/c020415a.asp.

Huotari, Maija-Leena, and T. D. Wilson. 2001. "Determining Organizational Information Needs: The Critical Success Factors Approach." *Informational Research* 6, no. 3: 10–14.

Kim, W. Chan, and Renée Mauborgne. 2005. *Blue Ocean Strategy.* Boston: Harvard Business School Press.

Labovitz, George. 1997. *The Power of Alignment.* Hoboken, NJ: John Wiley & Sons.

Roettger, Lloyd O., and Caroline Roettger. 2005. "Making Curriculum Sense Out of the Standards Movement or Driving School Improvement with Curriculum Designed Specifically for Continuous Improvement." Paper presented at the International Conference on Education. Honolulu, HI.

Part II

Tying the Fundamentals Together

11

Process Data: The Key to Knowing What Really Is Happening

OVERVIEW

Process data is a generic term for data collected regularly through a designated period. *Formative data* is a synonym for process data and is often used in education circles. Either term is satisfactory when educators are communicating with other educators. Process data, however, is a more appropriate term to use when educators are communicating with the public.

Why do people need process data? It is because they want to see improvement in the end-of-the-year results (summative) data. Process data provides feedback along the way in order to make adjustments as the year progresses. Ideally, the process data correlate perfectly with the results data so that there are no surprises in the results data. For example, if a state scores student writing on a 1–4 scale at the end of a school year, the hope would be that the monthly writing scores (process data) taken during the school year would produce the exact same results. When the process data are aligned with the results data, then teachers and administrators can make adjustments throughout the year with great confidence that the changes will positively affect the results.

How is process data collected? What data are collected? What display choices provide the most insight from the data?

First, it is important to conduct an examination of existing data to determine areas needing improvement. The collection and display of data (charts and graphs) should be undertaken for areas in need of improvement. If students are behaving in the cafeteria, there is no need to collect and display data on behavior in the cafeteria. Even if some adults believe that the cafeteria noise is too loud, if the students are eating, then the students are accomplishing the aim of lunch. Collection and display of data are necessary only when people see a need for improvement.

The second step in data collection is to determine the ideal or perfect situation. What is being determined is analogous to batting 1.000 in baseball, as described earlier in regard to Baldrige Criteria. Nobody expects to have a ball player who bats 1.000, but all know that batting 1.000 is perfect. In education, perfect would be no discipline referrals for the year, every student writes a level 4 paper on a scale of 1 to 4, and on weekly math quizzes, every student answers every question correctly. The reason for this determination is that the graphing of process data represents perfect results on the *y*-axis. The *x*-axis shows the number of times during the school year that data are collected. Figure 11.1 is a blank run chart for process data on school discipline. Zero is at the bottom of the *y*-axis because a week with no referrals is perfect. The *y*-axis in this school goes up to 25 because the very worst week the prior year had 25 referrals to the office. The *x*-axis runs from 1 to 37 because there are 36 or 37 weeks in the school year. Collecting data is simple; improving the results is not.

Step three is the simple step: count the number of discipline referrals to the office each week and graph the number. Display publicly. Step four is the hard part: determine what can be done to reduce the number of referrals to the office. The leader's job is to develop a hypothesis, based upon input from others, and test the hypothesis to see if it reduces the number of referrals.

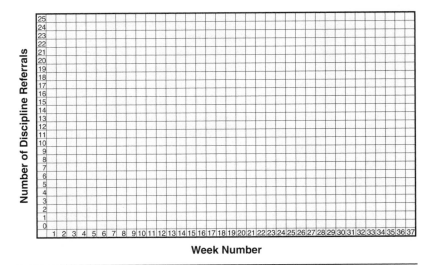

Figure 11.1 Process data for discipline referrals.

The above example provides an idea of how to collect and organize process data. In this example, the school is the unit for measurement. However, these same graphs can be used for the student as an individual, for the classroom, the grade level/department, or even the whole school district.

Other examples that may increase understanding are for improving writing, increasing reading fluency, and increasing the number of sit-ups performed. The hypothetical school for these examples has 500 students. For writing, each student is scored using a rubric, once a month. The y-axis on this graph goes to 2000 (every student scoring a 4 on a 1–4 scale) and the x-axis is either nine or 10 depending on how many months data are collected. In the reading fluency example, every student reads once per month for a minute and the words read correctly are totaled for the whole school. A school of 500 students has the possibility of reading 10,000 words in a minute. The sit-ups graph would look similar; however, the students will probably be unable to do as many sit-ups in a minute as they can read words in a minute.

Again, the easy part is the collecting and graphing of the data. Another important part of the process is congratulating the students on the increases in performance. The responsibility of the leader is to always be on the lookout for all-time-bests. It is easy to think of many ways to thank the students for their hard work. The students appreciate the thanks. They will take your money if you foolishly choose to reward them externally, but all they need is sincere appreciation for their hard work.

The hard part is continually increasing the learning. How do we increase the writing ability? The reading fluency? The physical fitness? The behavior? The significance of having process data is that everyone will know when the results are improving. The team is working together to bring about the improvement. The individual and collective evidence of learning provides the internal motivation that so many students lack.

Process data can be collected for aspects of schooling where it is a little more complicated to get a handle on all of the content. In *Improving Student Learning* (2002), an example is provided of Lee's first experience with process data in 1992–93. The collected data was the learning of 100 locations on a USA map throughout a fifth-grade year. There is not time to give the students a 100-item exam on geography every week, so a different method was employed. This different method includes the following steps:

1. Inform the students about the end-of-the-year expectations. In this case, provide the 100 locations on the U.S. map to students at the beginning of the school year.

2. Each week the students take a quiz on a sample of the locations. The items on the quizzes are selected randomly.

The recommended sample size is the square root of the total locations. Therefore, in the geography example the quiz includes 10 locations weekly.

3. Each student graphs the number correct each week. Most students have zero to two correct at the beginning of the year and will gradually increase to nine or 10 correct by the end of the year, if the curriculum is correctly aligned and the teaching is effective.

4. The teacher graphs the number of correct answers for the class as a whole. In the 1992 example, the teacher had 32 students so the class was working toward 320 correct.

5. Again, the hard part is how to increase the learning, not how to graph it.

For the leader of the school, the geography task is slightly different: how many locations, vocabulary words, and geographical principles does the whole school understand? The principal works with the teachers to reach agreement on geography expectations for each grade level, establishes the reporting process, and documents the school's improvement. Further, there is a graph for the school as a whole. The principal cannot leave each grade level alone to agree on expectations by themselves. This can cause duplication of information in multiple grade levels. Curriculum alignment is necessary. Further coordination between grade levels is necessary to be sure that students do not forget the content of prior grades. Two examples of grade-level coupling come from Rochester, Indiana. They agreed that spelling tests would be 10 words from the current grade level, four from the prior grade level, and two words from the grade level two years prior. In math, they agreed on seven concepts from the current grade level, two from the prior grade, and one from two years prior.

The exact formula does not matter; experience and logic provide the bases for the formula. For example, *their, there,* and *they're* might never be dropped from spelling lists, but carried forward into all future grades. The students would know that these three items are second-grade review words, not current-grade words. They would also know that they still have to remember these words from prior grades.

At the district level, process data gathering is similar. The difficulty with district-level leadership is aligning learning expectations from kindergarten through high school. To the best of our knowledge, no U.S. publisher publishes a K–12 set of textbooks. The high school geometry textbook, for example, may begin the year as if the students had no prior knowledge of geometry. However, students work with geometry concepts in grades K–9.

District-level leadership requires that geometry teachers know the content taught in K–9 and what content is new in grade 10. Once expectations are established and aligned, personnel can start collecting data on student learning, as shown in Figures 11.2 and 11.3.

The basic process data graphs are run charts, scatter diagrams, and histograms. Figure 11.3 is Mrs. Nowell's seventh-grade math class from Lee

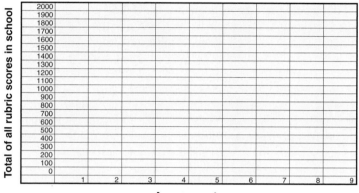

Figure 11.2 Run chart for school writing.

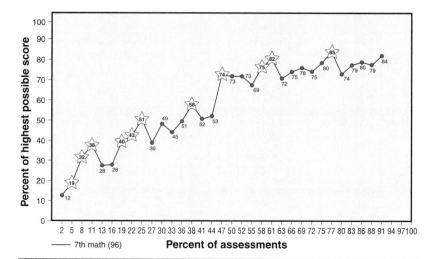

Figure 11.3 Class (percent) run chart for Mrs. Nowell's seventh-grade math classes.

Kornegay Junior High School (Miami, Arizona). Note the near continuous improvement as evidenced by 11 all-time-bests (starred items). Figure 11.4 is a score run chart from Mr. Wilson's 10th-grade American history classroom. (Note 12 all-time-bests with the peak coming the week before the state graduation test.) Figure 11.5 shows the combined class run charts of four kindergarten teachers at Los Lomas Elementary (Note nine all-time-bests) and Figure 11.6 is a scatter diagram of Miami High School's advanced biology course taught by Mr. Anthony, with a dot for each student each week of the school year; the diagonal line is the AYP goal. Figure 11.7 is an individual run chart as an overlay to the scatter diagram; the run charts and the scatter diagrams create a very complete picture of learning progress. Finally, when the curriculum is correctly aligned it will produce a three-part L to J histogram that depicts the L on the left, a bell curve in the center, and a J on the right. Figure 11.8 is such a depiction from Lloyd's graduate supervision class of correctly written and taught curriculum.

One final note: the major purpose of charting data is to manage continually the *aim* of the organization at all levels. This helps the team stay focused on the work, the results, and the all-time-best celebrations.

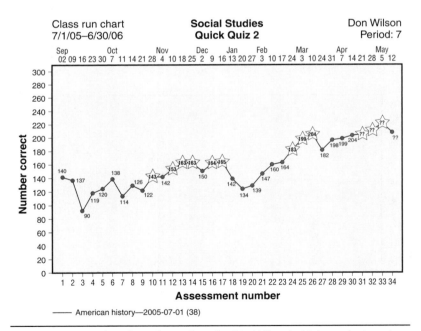

Figure 11.4   Student (score) run chart for Mr. Wilson's 10th-grade American history class.

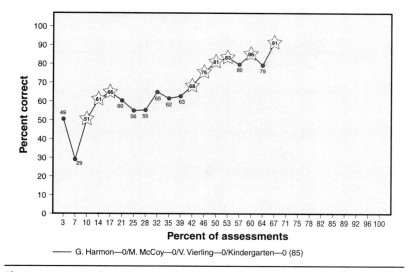

Figure 11.5   Kindergarten run chart—four classrooms.

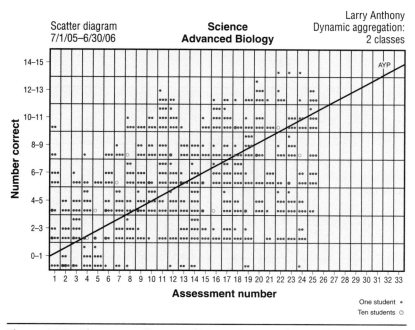

Figure 11.6   The scatter diagram of Mr. Anthony's advanced biology classes.

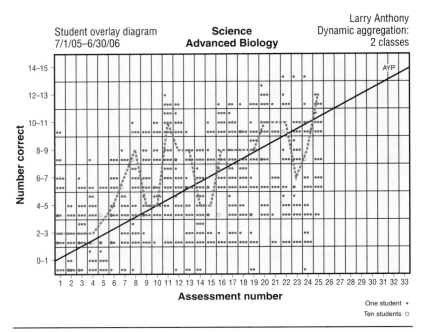

Figure 11.7   The individual run chart as an overlay to the scatter diagram of Mr. Anthony's advanced biology classes.

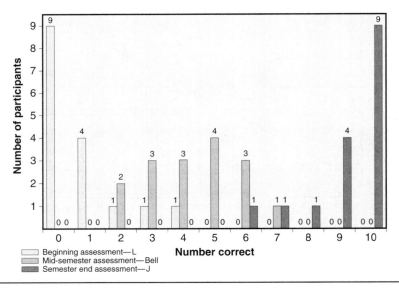

Figure 11.8   A depiction of correctly aligned curriculum.

Core Values

Management by fact that uses performance measurement to focus on improving student learning.

Focus on results and creating value as the means to improving student learning and building loyalty.

Learning-centered education that places the focus of education on learning and the real needs of students.

Baldrige Connection

Describe how your school identifies and manages its key processes for creating student and stakeholder value and maximizing student learning and success.

Measurement, analysis, and knowledge management serve as a foundation for the performance management system and are critical to the effective management of your school and to a fact-based, knowledge-driven system for improving performance.

Guiding Questions

What are the key performance measures or indicators used for the control and improvement of your learning-centered processes? How does your day-to-day operation of these processes ensure meeting key process requirements? How are in-process measures used in managing these processes? How do you incorporate a measurement plan that makes effective use of formative and summative assessment? How is student, stakeholder, faculty, staff, and partner input used in managing these processes, as appropriate?

Adapted from *2005 Education Criteria for Performance Excellence.*

RESOURCES AND REFERENCES

Ayres, Carolyn. 2000. *Continuous Improvement in the Mathematics Classroom.* Milwaukee: ASQ Quality Press.

Burgard, Jeff. 2000. *Continuous Improvement in the Science Classroom.* Milwaukee: ASQ Quality Press.

Carson, Shelly. 2000. *Continuous Improvement in the History/Social Science Classroom.* Milwaukee: ASQ Quality Press.

Fauss, Karen. 2000. *Continuous Improvement in the Primary Classroom.* Milwaukee: ASQ Quality Press.

From L to J Software. 2003. *Knowledge Power Software.* Scottsdale, AZ. www.knowledgepower.com.

Jenkins, Lee. 2002. *Improving Student Learning: Applying Deming's Quality Principles in Classrooms,* 2nd ed. Milwaukee: ASQ Quality Press.

12

Alignment: Unifying the Organization for Action

OVERVIEW

Joseph Juran (1992), an organizational expert who worked as a contemporary of Deming and recently celebrated his 100th birthday, stated that approximately one-third of what people do is re-doing work that has been already done. Why? Some of it is personal disorganization, but the preponderance is organizational disorganization. The term used in education for cleaning up the disorganization is *alignment*.

The most important alignment in education is alignment with each other. There are other alignment duties, but "with each other" is the primary responsibility of leaders. In a report on why some schools are so much more successful than others, researchers found "the bedrock foundation: this penetrating, deep understanding of what it is children are to know and be able to do and how to connect it across the grades." (Olson 2005)

It certainly seems that education would have this done. Every school district in every state should be able to provide any interested party the precise descriptions of what students are to know and be able to do for every grade level. Why is this not the case? There may be several answers, but clearly one answer is overreliance on textbooks as guides. One does not pick up the newspaper and read a horror story about a parent who went into a school and was unable to obtain the grade-level expectations. What one does read is that a parent went into a school and found that the school was short of textbooks.

It is clear, however, that textbook publishers are unable to align curriculum. It is beyond their ability to come to each town and help the teachers and administrators align their expectations with each other and then publish accordingly. When we write about aligning with each other, we mean alignment from kindergarten through grade 12.

One reason that teachers, administrators, students, and parents do not have this penetrating, deep understanding of what children are to know and be able to do is that the alignment documents are often five times larger than necessary. Why? Because often each learning expectation is included in five different grades. A particular concept is first introduced in grade 3, reintroduced in grade 4, "mastered" in grade 5, reviewed in grade 6, and reinforced in grade 7. This paper-wasting process of writing down each concept five times creates a document that teachers find overwhelming and students never see. We recommend that school districts write down each essential concept in only one grade level. Each teacher has the primary responsibility for students to learn the concepts for their grade level. Next, the document should have a preface stating that teachers have the responsibility to introduce the topics of two future grades and review two prior grade levels in addition to their primary responsibility of "mastery" of grade-level content. Districts need to assist teachers with the definition of "introduce." What does this mean?

Introducing content has different meanings for different subjects. In history, for example, "introduce" could mean that teachers read students a historical fiction novel from the period to be studied one or two years in the future. In mathematics, it almost certainly means to have students use manipulatives for the concept. For example, if add/subtract/multiply/divide fractions is a fifth-grade expectation, then third- and fourth-grade students can use *Fraction Tiles* (McLean and Jenkins 1973) or other manipulatives for the four operations prior to abstract explanations in grade five.

What does *reinforce* mean? Teachers need definitions and examples. A reinforcement example for fractions might be assigning students the question, "What fractional part of our campus is covered with grass?"

An alignment of both sides of the curriculum house—what students know and what they can do—is necessary. Two examples that demonstrate this are writing and reading fluency. The use of writing rubrics to assess writing ability is acceptable from kindergarten to grade 12. There should be increased expectations at every grade. In general, the higher levels of the rubric at one grade level become the lower levels for the next grade level. In reading fluency, the double task is to agree on text difficulty and reading speed for each grade level.

Communicate with parents and students the expectations for as many as five grade levels at once—two prior grade levels, current grade, and two future grade levels. A simple example is giving third graders the first-

and second-grade spelling words (for review), the third-grade spelling (for learning this year), and the fourth- and fifth-grade spelling (for curiosity and setting the stage for the future).

One final note: Alignment of curriculum is an ongoing process. The clarity of what is to be taught helps teachers and students reach higher levels of success. As this occurs, a reevaluation of the curriculum occurs in order to assure that the students are working at the highest level possible. This creates new all-time-bests each year.

Core Value

Systems perspective that provides a keen understanding of alignment as a strategy for improving the overall school.

Baldrige Connection

The term "alignment" refers to consistency of plans, processes, information, resource decisions, actions, results, and analysis to support key schoolwide goals. Effective alignment requires a common understanding of purposes and goals. It also requires the use of complementary measures and information for planning, tracking, analysis, and improvement at three levels: the organizational level/senior leader level, the key process level, and the program, school, class, or individual level.

Guiding Questions

Describe the alignment and integration in your performance management system. For example, when you identify key strategic objectives, your action plans, faculty and staff development plans, some of your performance measures, and some results should be expected to relate to the stated strategic objectives.

Adapted from *2005 Education Criteria for Performance Excellence.*

RESOURCES AND READING LIST

Juran, Joseph M. 1992. *Juran on Quality by Design: The New Steps for Planning Quality into Goods and Services.* New York: The Free Press, 2.

McLean, Peggy, and Lee Jenkins. 1973. *Fraction Tiles.* Hayward, CA: Activity Resources.

Olson, Lynn. 2005. "Sleuths Seek Secrets of High-Flying Schools." *Education Week* 24, no. 34.

13

Starting: Looking for the Missing Link in Leading for Continuous Improvement

OVERVIEW

This is not a chapter on documenting the teachers who are in the wrong profession. It is about assisting teachers as they aspire to meet the needs of a larger and larger percentage of students. In order for people to improve they need advice from customers, peers, and bosses (to use generic terms). Teachers need feedback from students and parents, and we earlier described the plus/delta as one effective tool for eliciting this feedback. Another feedback method is asking students to fill out a survey such as the one designed by Cottrell (see Appendix A). Next, there is help from peers and mentors. Teachers should regularly visit and be visited by other teachers. The joy of observing others teach should not be limited to administrators.

In this chapter, however, we are not discussing student/parent or peer assistance, but administrator assistance. Teachers desire to have administrators who are both visible and helpful. The following process can assist both teachers and administrators as they strive to use effective communication as a vehicle for improved teaching.

Improving instruction in today's educational system requires a mutual effort between teachers and school leaders. The process described in this chapter is one way of accomplishing continuous improvement in the classroom. It is the school leader's responsibility to create a relationship with teachers. The result is a climate that fosters shared efforts to improve teaching and learning. The collaboration of teachers and administrators in developing effective teaching methods is often a missing link in leadership. The process shared here is one that allows administrators to coach for growth by meeting frequently with teachers to discuss and investigate instructional improvement strategies. This is a nonevaluative process. It also allows teachers the freedom to experiment, to be mentored by the administrator, and to be a full and equal partner in deciding how to approach and deploy instruction. Every teacher faces the same dilemma: the desire to get better versus the desire to get good ratings. For the school leader, the aim of instructional leadership is to improve performance. To be effective at meeting this aim, a school leader needs to be trusted and have credibility as an instructional improvement specialist. Building trust and credibility requires being able to identify effective teaching behaviors and giving teachers helpful ideas or suggestions as to how to use these behaviors. This support can come as a result of skilled classroom observation, the analysis of lesson designs/ classroom structures, and judicious recording and reporting of job performance. The delivery of the recommendation is most effective when quality, face-to-face conferences are held with the teacher, and growth goals and strategies are mutually constructed to assist in guiding the teacher's journey to excellence in teaching. Effective teacher performance improvement (TPI) has the power to become a catalyst for continuously improving the processes of teaching and learning. In fact, the connection between giving teachers the instructional leadership to get better and teachers continuously improving instructional practices is necessary to help all teachers do the best they can.

How does an administrator find the time to be an instructional leader? It should be built into the leader's daily schedule. A specific time each day should be allotted for instructional work, and during this time, the administrator should be free from interruptions, unless an emergency exists. This schedule is available to all constituents of the school. Since the principal is the instructional leader of the school, it should make sense that the leader makes time to be in the school working with teachers and students every day.

The process is simple and cyclical (see Figure 13.1). The cycle is a formative (coaching) process and is in no way an evaluation from the principal.

The aim of the cycle is to coach, mentor, and assist the teacher for improvement. Even great teachers will tell you there is something they would like to do better. The process is a nonjudgmental sharing of data about teaching decisions made relative to a teacher's lesson. The teaching episode is observed and data is gathered using either the wide lens of an entire lesson or the narrow lens of specific elements. The objectives of data recording are to be able to record data that will enable the school leader to analyze instructional decisions, to analyze the efficacy of teaching strategies and techniques, and to provide specific, valid advice. This advice should provide answers to questions such as:

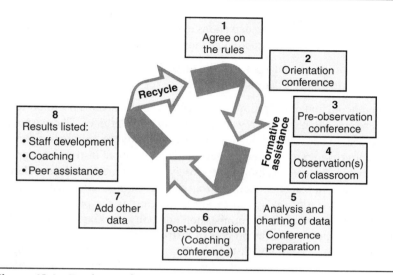

Figure 13.1 Teacher performance improvement cycle.

- Was the lesson/activity design effective?

- What methods, strategies, or elements contributed most to lesson/ activity effectiveness?

- What did the teacher do that could really make a difference if done better or more frequently?

- What, if any, are the methods, strategies, or elements that really need to be worked on or eliminated?

- What methods, strategies, or elements, if improved, would make the lesson more effective?

- What hypothesis was being tested?

- Were there any behaviors or strategies that are worthy of discussion?

- To what extent was the lesson effective?

- What was done to meet the objective(s), when, and for how long?

- To what extent were the students task-oriented and appeared to feel comfortable about interacting with the teacher and each other?

- To what extent were the students engaged by the instructional strategy?

- What charts or other depictions evident in the classroom present an environment of continuous improvement?

- What specific anecdotal, scripted, or charted data support the administrator's decisions?

Conferencing for collaboration with teachers is perhaps the most important, challenging, complex, and rewarding activity a leader does. The purposes of the conference are to recognize quality performance, reinforce specific areas for growth, provide needed help, collaborate about instructional practices, and let the persons know how closely they are meeting the standards of excellence in teaching. Deming was clear about his belief that continuous improvement of the system requires working on the processes within that system. Teachers and administrators mutually working for the benefit of students can improve the process of instruction.

The process begins with the teacher and school leader developing a mutually agreed upon set of rules for the process. The most critical understanding is that it has nothing to do with the summative evaluation of the teacher. The school leader cannot do this intensive assistance process with more than five to 10 teachers. The best process is to take about a third of the teachers each year to include "on cycle."

If a three-year cycle is implemented, one possibility is to use formal student/parent feedback such as in Appendix A for year 1, a formal peer review process in year 2, and the administrator process described in this chapter in year 3.

The next step is to provide a complete orientation to the teachers "on cycle" by meeting with them individually to discuss their personal learning plan and identify the areas where the school leader can provide the most help. A schedule of visits should include walk-throughs, short observations, focused specific visits, and longer full-lesson observations. The third step in the cycle is a preobservation conference 24 to 48 hours before the teaching episode. The school leader should provide the teacher with a guide page so that he or she can express the following information:

- Identify the topic(s): new, review, or diagnostic?

- Which of the essential elements of a teaching episode are appropriate for this lesson/activity? What are the plans? Cottrell's research indicates that excellent teachers vary their use of the elements, but always include checking for understanding.

  – Anticipatory set

  – Instructional objective: essential facts, learnings, and concepts

- Content input: teaching methods and procedures

- Modeling: demonstration

- Checking for understanding: monitoring and adjusting

- Guided practice: in-class supervision

- Independent practice: work at home

- Closure

- Discuss any unique or unusual characteristics of the students in the class to be observed.

- Identify the teaching behavior(s) to be monitored.

The typical format of the preobservation conference is to discuss the lesson, establish the ground rules for the observation, and set up specific times and plans for carrying out the observation. During the observation, the administrator will script anecdotes and verbal behaviors to discuss with the teacher in the postobservation conference. Step five is to do a thorough analysis of the data gathered in the observation. Some questions to use in the planning of the postconference include the following:

- How can I best help the teacher?

- Have I the data to provide specific advice?

- What are the teacher's building blocks (things they do well)?

- What are the teacher's targets for growth (things they could do better)?

- Have I considered the style and needs of the teacher?

- Have I planned ways to involve the teacher and increase collaboration?

- What percent of students gave evidence of learning? Which students gave evidence of not learning either through boredom or confusion?

The postconference is held within 72 hours of the observation. During the postobservation conference, the teacher and administrator can discuss the observed teacher behaviors, building blocks, and targets for growth. In addition, they can make plans for future observations. Steps 3, 4, 5, and 6 are repeated several times throughout the year. Also short, focused observations provide information and specific advice about one of the essential elements. Mutual problem solving, collaboration, and coaching for growth are good ways to foster continuous improvement in instruction.

It is easy to see why time for instructional leadership must be in the daily schedule. Intensive coordination between administrator and teacher can not occur in a haphazard manner. Planning is essential and daily interaction with teachers and instruction are necessary. This work is one way to build the relationships that are necessary for continuous improvement to occur.

Core Values

Management by fact that uses performance measurement to focus on improving teacher performance.

Valuing faculty, staff, and partners by leadership who is not only dependent upon but committed to the knowledge, skills, innovative creativity, and motivation of its workforce.

Organizational and personal learning that is directed not only toward better educational programs, services and teaching, but also toward being more flexible, adaptive, and responsive to the needs of students and stakeholders.

Baldrige Connection

The term "summative assessment" refers to longitudinal analysis of the learning and performance of teachers and staff. Summative assessments tend to be formal and comprehensive, and they often cover global performance and behavior. Such assessments may be conducted at anytime during the school year or at the conclusion of a course or program and could be compared to the results of previous assessments to determine improvement or gains and to clarify the causal connections between educational practices and student learning. They may be used for purposes of determining continuing contracts, tenure, promotion, and pay for performance as well as for licensure or certification. The term "formative assessment" refers to frequent or ongoing evaluation during courses, programs, or learning experiences that allows for early indications of how teachers and staff are performing and allows for continuous improvement through feedback.

Guiding Questions

What are your key performance measures or indicators used for the control and improvement of your learning-centered processes? How does your day-to-day operation of these processes ensure meeting key process requirements? How do you incorporate a measurement plan that

---

Continued

Continued

makes effective use of formative and summative assessment? How does your faculty and staff formative evaluation system, including feedback to faculty and staff, support high-performance work and contribute to the achievement of your action plans? How does your faculty and staff formative evaluation system support a student and stakeholder focus? How do your compensation, recognition, and related reward and incentive practices reinforce high-performance work and a student and stakeholder focus? How do you contribute to faculty and staff learning and motivate your faculty and staff? How do you identify characteristics and skills of faculty and staff? How do you ensure you're your faculty and staff are continuously improving? How do you accomplish effective succession planning for leadership and supervisory positions? How do you manage effective career progression for all faculty and staff throughout the district? How do you ensure faculty and staff are appropriately certified or licensed?

Adapted from *2005 Education Criteria for Performance Excellence.*

RESOURCES AND READING LIST

Danielson, Charlotte, and Thomas L. McGreal. 2000. *Teacher Evaluation: To Enhance Professional Practice.* Alexandria, VA: ASCD.

Kise, Jane A. G. 2006. *Differentiated Coaching : A Framework for Helping Teachers Change.* Thousand Oaks, CA: Corwin Press.

McGrath, Mary Jo. 2002. "The Lead with S.U.C.C.E.E.D. Program." McGrath Training Systems. Santa Barbara, CA.

14

Experimentation: The Key to Getting It Right

OVERVIEW

"Managers must see themselves as experimenters who lead learning, not dictators who impose control." This statement sums up this chapter very well. Scholtes continues, "Most managerial dictums are hypotheses. A hypothesis by nature is useless unless proven by data" (Scholtes 1998).

Employees would be much more agreeable if their bosses would merely state, "I have a hypothesis regarding what might fix the problem we are facing. I do not know for sure if it will work, but have found that other organizations have been successful with this solution. That does not mean it will work for us, or that it is even the best solution. We are going to test out the concept in one locale, see if it works, and if it does, we will consider a wider implementation." Instead of this, employees often have bosses who are unwilling to admit that their idea is a hypothesis and instead present their concept as a solution. The problem employees have is that the vast majority of the past "solutions" have either not worked or were discarded by a new boss.

A school system was studying payroll errors. A calculation of errors per month over a three-year period determined that the number of errors was consistent at six to eight per month. Further study found that the majority of errors were with pay for substitutes. Errors were coming into the payroll office; the payroll office itself was not making the errors. The recipient of the check with the error assumed that the error came from the payroll office, but this was not the case. One secretary knew of a method another school district employed that might solve this problem, and an experiment was set for one year in one school. The error rate from the one school greatly improved, so the next year all schools used the new plan. The errors for the school district decreased to an average of one per month with districtwide implementation.

This is what Scholtes addresses. The leader of the school system had several choices in regard to the payroll problem:

1. Blame the payroll office and document errors in personnel files.

2. Blame the school secretaries who sent the incorrect information to the payroll office.

3. Ignore the advice of the one secretary.

4. Accept the advice of the one secretary and make the suggestion to implement the new policy immediately.

5. Lead the effort to conduct an experiment to see if the suggestion will work. Only if the experiment shows positive results will implementation occur in all schools.

This fifth choice is the focus of this chapter.

The confidence to conduct experiments comes from a deep inner belief on the part of the leader that the cause of most problems in an organization is a system error, not an individual people error. Yes, people do make errors, and organizations do have "porcupine" employees, which according to Collins (2001) is an employee who has many good points, but is tough to be around. However, the cause of most problems is the attitude that "the way we do things around here now is just fine." If the same problems occur repeatedly, then a change in the system is required. It takes a leader, who can facilitate the organization to become a hypothesis-testing organization, to lead permanent system change.

Darren Overton, principal of Pine Island Middle School in Pine Island, Minnesota, conducted an experiment during the 2005–06 school year regarding the correlation between adult/student relationships and letter grades. Each of the 400 students in his 5–8 school was listed on chart paper. Teachers placed a dot beside the name of each student they knew something about, other than academics. This could be sports, hobbies, family, church, or even family responsibilities. The grade point average for students was compared with the number of dots (five or more dots, four dots, three dots, two dots, one dot, and zero dots) for each student. The grade point averages for the six groups amazingly showed a 100 percent correlation between each student's GPA and the number of dots on the teacher's chart. The experiment: Teachers were asked to develop a close relationship with students who had zero or one dot. The idea is to see if the students do better in school (discipline and academics both) when somebody takes time to show a real interest in them. The reason for telling this story is not to have every reader conduct the same experiment, but to give an example of leadership experimentation. (The June 2006 results show the hypothesis was correct as the school had its all-time-best in office referrals for the sixth year in a row.)

The leader needs to be the chief person testing out hypotheses and the chief person encouraging teachers to test out hypotheses. Another hypothesis tested by teachers was, "Do students write better with 100 percent inspection of every writing assignment or do they write better with five papers selected at random from each writing assignment, a tally made of errors, and then lessons taught to meet common deficiencies?" In elementary grades, the experiment was with five papers from each teacher at a grade level. The item analysis was for the whole grade level. At the secondary level, the five sample papers were selected from each period taught by a particular teacher. The results from these experiments was higher state writing results and a "J" curve on school assessments.

Deming estimates that 95 percent of the changes made in organizations do not result in improvement. We would suggest that this is because no time is taken to test hypotheses before a change is dictated.

One more key recommendation from Deming is to recognize that it only takes one example contrary to one's theory to require revisiting the theory. For example, many schools operate from the theory that students are more likely to graduate from high school if they take all required courses their ninth-grade year. However, all eighth- and ninth-grade teachers know that at least one ninth-grader is not mature enough to handle all required courses. What should we do? Nobody knows for sure. This is a time for experiments to see what works best.

Once a leader internalizes the concept that one example contrary to one's theory requires revisiting the theory, the leader will continually test theories in order to improve the system. Another theory in high schools that requires testing is the starting time for school. Would more students graduate if they could attend school from 10:00 to 5:00 instead of 8:00 to 3:00? We recognize that the whole high school cannot change its schedule. However, all a high school needs is a couple of teachers who would volunteer to teach the 10 to 5 schedule to test the theory.

One of our favorite examples of testing hypotheses in a classroom comes from Jeff Burgard, author, teacher, and consultant. The first day of school, a complete list of key concepts was provided to his students that included what they were to learn in eighth-grade science. The students were quizzed and the results graphed, as described in Chapter 11. During the year, student learning stagnated, which caused the graph to flatline. Jeff asked his students, "What do you think we can do to raise our graph? What are your hypotheses?" The students landed on the hypothesis, "If we sit by our friends, the graph will go up." Jeff agreed that they could test the hypothesis for three weeks. Three weeks later, the students said, "Mr. Burgard, that didn't work. Put us where you want us." The two reasons this is one of our favorite examples are (1) the students were able to establish and carry out experiments on their learning and (2) it didn't work. So often we read about hypotheses that work and then may falsely assume that everybody else's theories always check out.

One final point: In order to improve continually, it is important to develop a positive way of looking at a problem. Education spends too much time discussing problems that can not be changed. This is a waste of valuable time. After these problems are identified, it is important to say, "These are things outside of our control; how can we change what is within our control to improve the situation? Focusing on the things we can do and then doing them, testing hypotheses and improving continually, creates an atmosphere of continual improvement, which results in building a culture of all-time-bests.

Core Values

Visionary leadership that creates and balances value for students and stakeholders.

Managing for innovation by making meaningful change to improve a school's programs, services, processes, and operations, and to create new value for the school's stakeholders.

Baldrige Connection

Describe how your school is led and managed so that experimentation and innovation become part of the learning culture. Achieving the highest levels of organizational performance requires a well-executed approach to organizational and personal learning. Organizational learning includes both continuous improvement of existing approaches and significant change, leading to new goals and approaches.

Guiding Questions

Does experimentation in pursuit of innovation lead your school to new dimensions of performance? Experimentation and innovation are no longer strictly the purview of research; they are important for providing ever-improving educational value to students and for improving all educational and operational processes.

Adapted from *2005 Education Criteria for Performance Excellence.*

RESOURCES AND READING LIST

Collins, Jim. 2001. *Good to Great: Why Some Companies Make the Leap . . . and Others Don't.* New York: Harper Collins.

Deming, W. Edwards. 1986. *Out of the Crisis.* Cambridge, MA: MIT Center for Advanced Engineering Study.

———. 1994. *The New Economics for Industry, Government, Education,* 2nd ed. Cambridge, MA: MIT Center for Advanced Engineering Study.

Jenkins, Lee. 2004. *Permission to Forget: And Nine Other Root Causes of America's Frustration with Education,* (Chapter 6). Milwaukee: ASQ Quality Press.

Scholtes, Peter. 1998. *The Leadership Handbook: Making Things Happen, Getting Things Done.* New York: McGraw Hill.

15

Barrier Removal: The Key to Enabling Success to Actually Happen

OVERVIEW

In, *The Knowing–Doing Gap: How Smart Companies Turn Knowledge into Action,* Pfeffer and Sutton (2000) wrote more than 300 pages on barrier removal. Why was this so important in the minds and research of these authors? It is because organizations rarely are able to implement what they know. The gap between what we know should occur and what actually occurs is wide in most businesses. In fact, Pfeffer and Sutton state that the professors in the schools of business, who later achieve leadership positions in corporations, do not lead the way they were teaching others to lead. Their research documents why it is so difficult to do what we know we should do.

If one were to interview 1000 teachers regarding why they became a teacher, it is doubtful any would say that their professional life goal was to assist students with their short-term memory. Their aspirations are to affect students' whole lives. Yet, teachers consistently give chapter tests, which are measures of short-term memory. Why this disconnect? One reason is the force of culture. When confronted with this dissonance between what teachers believe and what they do, the reply is often, "I have to put grades in the grade book—two per week is the board policy." Removal of board policies that are barriers should occur for systems to improve.

This chapter may well be the most important one in our book because all the other chapters are written to increase (or remind people) of knowledge. Pfeffer and Sutton (2000) write persuasively that increased knowledge is not enough. The knowledge must become action. Maybe as much time should be spent on developing strategies for barrier removal as is spent gaining knowledge.

The intent of the force-field analysis tool (Figure 15.1), described in Chapter 2, is to bring the barriers to the forefront. On the left side of the page, people write all the reasons why implementation of the new knowledge should occur. On the right side, people list the barriers to implementation. The line down the middle of the page represents status quo. In most organizations, there is a balance between the reasons for implementation and the reasons to avoid implementation (barriers). This produces the status quo. If leaders add pressure by adding a line to the left side of the ledger, then employees add a new listing on the right side to maintain the status quo. Leaders keep adding pressure and employees keep on adding reasons why the new knowledge will not work. It takes a lot of energy, on everyone's part, to maintain the status quo. Sometimes critics from outside a particular organization look at the status quo and assume it is because of laziness. Often this is not the case; tremendous energy is necessary to maintain the balance between new knowledge and barriers.

The removal of these barriers takes knowledge. A caution here is to avoid reliance on the personality of the leader. Sometimes leaders possess such a great personality, or charisma, that the employees go along with the new knowledge to please the leader. However, when this leader leaves, everything returns to the original state. The permanent removal of barriers occurs only with knowledge. This knowledge comes from listening. The staff knows the barriers and they understand that only the leaders can remove the barriers.

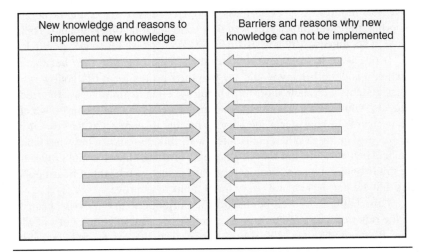

Figure 15.1   Force-field analysis.

In education, teachers are well aware that the administrators are the only ones that can remove the barriers keeping the organization from implementing best practices. However, these same teachers do not often think of themselves as leaders—leaders of a classroom. They have the same opportunity to remove barriers within the classroom that the principal has to remove schoolwide barriers, the superintendent has to remove districtwide barriers, the state department has to remove state barriers, and the federal government has to remove federal barriers.

When asked what the barriers are, people often reply, "a lack of time." John Conyers, the very successful superintendent of Community School District #15 in Palatine, Illinois, and winner of the Malcolm Baldrige National Quality Award was determined to remove some of the time barriers in his district (personal communication). He had each of his staff members describe exactly what it took to prepare for a board meeting and the time for each task. They presented this to the school board and the board stated that this was not how they wanted people spending their time. A change from two meetings per month to one meeting per month occurred. Further, he asked teachers to list all district requirements. A compiling of each teacher's list into one list for all teachers and an analysis by the district office staff determined the actual requirements. Staff were amazed at what they thought was required that really was not required.

Steve Lyng, while principal of Rochester High School (Indiana) established an "Education Garage Sale" with his staff as a means of removing barriers. The staff organized school practices into one of four categories:

1. *Send to museum.* These practices no longer serve the school well. Give them a place of honor and discontinue their use.

2. *Not for sale.* Must remain in the system.

3. *To be sold.* Still useful, but could be replaced with improved version.

4. *Garbage can.* These items do not work and may even be detrimental to the system.

Leaders could remove a huge barrier in special education. The barrier is for special education students receiving resource assistance one or two periods per day. The special education credential is, to a large degree, about alternative teaching strategies. The purpose of special education is to assist teachers with every possible tool to help the most difficult students succeed in school. When administrators go into these special education resource rooms, they should observe a myriad of tools being employed. Can they make this observation? Generally not. What is observed are special education resource teachers assisting special education students with their homework from their general education classes. The question is, why, with all of the teaching strategies in the heads of special education teachers, do they utilize mostly one method—homework? The reason is that the resource teachers are locked into homework as the primary method for teaching because a lack of homework produces F's for the student. A removal of this barrier by general education teachers is necessary. They need to say to their special education colleagues, "Here is what I want all my students to know by the end of the year and attached is what I want all students to be able to do at year's end. I absolutely do not care which method you use to help our shared students learn this material. I assign homework and you are free to use it as one of your tools. However, I know you have many other methods you can use. All are okay by me; just help them meet the standards. If they meet the standards, you do not need to worry about grades. The students will not be punished because you used a method other than homework."

We mentioned earlier that the knowledge to remove barriers comes from listening. Some will be informal listening, but much of the knowledge comes from formal listening, as in the Conyers examples.

Core Values

Visionary leadership that creates and balances value for students and stakeholders.

Agility with an explicit focus on faster and more flexible responses to needs of students and stakeholders.

Baldrige Connection

Removing barriers might require building community support and aligning community and business leaders and community services with this aim. Describe how attention is given to creating a learning environment that encourages ethical behavior and high performance.

Guiding Questions

How are learning barriers promptly identified and addressed? How does your school overcome barriers to teacher productivity and student success? How do school leaders remove barriers to guide and sustain your school, and accomplish the organizational vision, values, and performance expectations.

Adapted from *2005 Education Criteria for Performance Excellence.*

RESOURCES AND READING LIST

Conyers, John C., and Robert Ewy. 2003. *Charting Your Course.* Milwaukee: ASQ Quality Press.

Jenkins, Lee. 2004. *Permission to Forget: And Nine Other Root Causes of America's Frustration with Education,* (Chapter 4). Milwaukee: ASQ Quality Press.

Pheffer, Jeffrey, and Robert I. Sutton. 2000. *The Knowing–Doing Gap: How Smart Companies Turn Knowledge into Action.* Boston: The Harvard Business School Press.

16

Motivation of Others: Mission Impossible

OVERVIEW

Scholtes (1997), in *The Leader's Handbook: Making Things Happen, Getting Things Done,* considers the premise that we can motivate others as the ultimate in arrogance. He reminds us that the animal between the carrot and the stick is a jackass and when others attempt to motivate us with the carrot and the stick they are thinking of us as this very same animal. According to Covey (2004), the Industrial Age provides: "our carrot-and-stick motivational philosophy—the Great Jackass technique that motivates with a carrot in front (reward) and drives with a stick from behind (fear and punishment)." The problem is, managers today are still applying the Industrial Age control model to knowledge workers.

Deming's (1994) clear thinking on motivation is:

1. People are born motivated

2. Adults demotivate

3. Most people, once discouraged, stay discouraged

These ideas can provide some clarification on the loss of motivation in education. A discussion with students will verify that this occurs. The line of questioning could include the following. Tell me about a subject you really dislike in school. When did you decide you did not like _____? Why did you dislike the subject or topic at this time? It will generally be an adult who caused the loss of motivation. Finally, ask if there was ever a time when they changed their mind about a subject they disliked and began to like it again. It is good that Deming said "most" because sometimes formerly discouraged people do restore their motivation for a particular topic or subject. For Lee it was mathematics. His 10th-grade geometry teacher convinced him that he hated mathematics even though it had been his favorite subject up to that point. Fortunately, during his fouth year of teaching, this was turned around and mathematics has been the love of his career, even resulting in 10 mathematics manipulatives publications beginning with *It's a Tangram World* first published in 1970.

Deci (1996) has published the definitive work on motivation entitled *Why We Do What We Do.* He clearly distinguishes between motivation and control. People often confuse the two, thinking they are motivating people when in actuality they are really controlling them. The three of us are highly motivated to learn and communicate. Money does not motivate us, but money does control our calendars. What we learned prior to writing this book and what we are learning as a result of this writing is purely intrinsic. However, we have teaching and speaking calendars for which we are paid. The money controls the calendar, but not one whit of the motivation.

So, when supervisors read this book, it may be a shock to their systems to read that they cannot motivate their employees. They can, to a certain extent, control them with money and the fear of a loss of money, but they cannot motivate them.

The job of supervisors, and this includes teachers, who are the managers of students, is to maintain the level of motivation at entry. For bosses in business, this means to keep the motivation as high as it was when the employees first began their work. One source of information regarding motivation comes from employees. If employees never recommend that their friends come work with them, it is a good sign of an unmotivated employee.

When considering motivation, it is helpful to understand that leaders have only three assets: knowledge, personality, and positional power. Everyone wants their supervisors to first use knowledge in day-to-day operations, secondly use their personality, and last of all use power. People do not like working for bosses that start with power, occasionally use personality, and have absolutely no knowledge. Leaders should use all three assets. After knowledge, personality is a help. Further, all leaders must use power on occasion.

Many educators have been given terrible advice: motivate your students to learn. Why is this so harmful? It is because students come to kindergarten already motivated. They do not need motivation. It is the responsibility of educators to maintain the incoming level of motivation. Educators and other bosses are to find out why students and employees are losing their motivation and stop such practices. This is hard work. It is much simpler to throw out a bonus, a few stickers, or a few points toward grades. Listening to what causes the loss of motivation, and then actually doing something about it—that is hard work.

One final note: introducing fear into an organization is probably the greatest demotivator. Deming was very clear about this. It is the responsibility of leaders to drive fear out of the organization.

IMPLEMENTATION STEPS

1. Publicly admit that you, as leader, cannot motivate others

2. Gather baseline data on motivation with a survey

3. Use listening tools to remove barriers to high motivation

4. Repeat baseline data collection on an annual basis

5. The use of a climate study will provide excellent baseline data

TOOLS FOR ANNUAL SURVEY OF STUDENT MOTIVATION

Happy Face Survey

Directions: Check a happy face, straight face, or sad face for school and then for each school subject

	Happy	Straight	Sad
School	☺	😐	☹
Reading	☺	😐	☹
History	☺	😐	☹
Geography	☺	😐	☹
Art	☺	😐	☹
Science	☺	😐	☹
Math	☺	😐	☹
Writing	☺	😐	☹
Music	☺	😐	☹
Physical Education	☺	😐	☹

Employee Survey

Directions: Check never, seldom, 50/50, most of time, or almost always

	Never	Seldom	50/50	Most of time	Almost always
I love teaching	❏	❏	❏	❏	❏
I love staff meetings	❏	❏	❏	❏	❏
I love district staff development	❏	❏	❏	❏	❏
I love my grade-level meetings	❏	❏	❏	❏	❏
I love my department meetings	❏	❏	❏	❏	❏
I love meeting outside my grade level	❏	❏	❏	❏	❏
I love conferences	❏	❏	❏	❏	❏
I love parent/teacher conferences	❏	❏	❏	❏	❏

EDUCATION EXAMPLE

John Conyers, Palatine, Illinois, superintendent, stated that his district always scored in the 80th percentile, unable to crack the 90th percentile. It was not until he implemented the student enthusiasm strategies described by Burgard and Carson that they were able to move above the 90th percentile. There were other activities teachers added to stop the loss of enthusiasm, but the core knowledge was in the two books by Burgard and Carson.

Core Values

Organizational and personal learning. Achieving the highest levels of organizational performance requires a well-executed approach to organizational and personal learning.

Valuing faculty, staff, and partners. A school's success depends increasingly on the diverse backgrounds, knowledge, skills, creativity, and motivation of all its faculty, staff, and partners.

Baldrige Connection

Describe how learning is directed not only toward better educational programs and services but also toward being more adaptive, innovative, flexible, and responsive to the needs of students, stakeholders, and the market, as well as giving your faculty and staff satisfaction and motivation to excel. Describe how your school's work systems and faculty and staff learning and motivation enable faculty and staff to develop and utilize their full potential in alignment with your school's overall objectives, strategy, and action plans. What are your school's efforts to build and maintain a work environment and faculty and staff support climate conducive to performance excellence and to personal and organizational growth?

Guiding Questions

How do you determine the key factors that affect student well-being, satisfaction, and motivation? How do you motivate faculty and staff to develop and utilize their full potential? How do you organize and manage work and jobs, including skills, to promote cooperation, initiative, empowerment, innovation, and your organizational culture? How do you reinforce the use of new knowledge and skills on the job and retain this knowledge for long-term organizational use?

Adapted from *2005 Education Criteria for Performance Excellence.*

RESOURCES AND READING LIST

Burgard, Jeff. 2000. *Continuous Improvement in the Science Classroom,* (Chapter 8). Milwaukee: ASQ Quality Press.

Carson, Shelly. 2000. *Continuous Improvement in the History/Social Science Classroom,* (Chapter 2). Milwaukee: ASQ Quality Press.

Conyers, John C., and Robert Ewy. 2003. *Charting Your Course.* Milwaukee: ASQ Quality Press.

Covey, Stephen R. 2004. *The Eighth Habit.* New York: The Free Press.

Deci, Edward L. 1996. *Why We Do What We Do: Understanding Self-Motivation.* New York: Penguin Press.

Deming, W. Edwards. 1986. *Out of the Crisis.* Cambridge, MA: MIT Center for Advanced Engineering Study.

―――. 1994. *The New Economics for Industry, Government, Education,* 2nd ed. Cambridge, MA: MIT Center for Advanced Engineering Study.

Jenkins, Lee. 2003. *Improving Student Learning: Applying Deming's Quality Principles in Classrooms,* 2nd ed. Milwaukee: ASQ Quality Press.

―――. 2004. *Permission to Forget,* (Chapter 8). Milwaukee: ASQ Quality Press.

Jenkins, Lee, and Peggy McLean. 1970. *It's a Tangram World.* Hayward, CA: Activity Resources.

Scholtes, Peter, R. 1997. *The Leader's Handbook: Making Things Happen, Getting Things Done.* New York: McGraw-Hill.

17

True Improvement: Addressing Root Causes Once and For All

OVERVIEW

Every problem is a "why" or a "who" problem. Dr. Deming was quoted, late in his life, as saying from 94 percent up to 97 percent of life's problems are "why" problems, not "who" problems. This is a central, key understanding in leadership. Leaders need not do anything but answer the phone or accept appointments to hear of problems.

The first reaction of leaders should be "Why did this happen?" not "Who did this to us?" That is a big switch in the thinking of U.S. citizens. This book is being written while Hurricane Katrina is still in the news. Much of the news has been about blame instead of why. Few newspaper articles are published on why. One article in *USA Today* hypothesized that hurricanes are hitting cities with more force than before because there is less land between the gulf shores and cities. The next question is "Why less land?" The answer was that the land is being washed away by gulf shore waves on the coastline. The next question is "Is this a new problem, and if so, why is it occurring?" The hypothesis is that the Mississippi is carrying less silt and soil into the delta to replace lost land. "Why is the Mississippi carrying less silt and soil?" The hypothesis is because of dams on the Mississippi.

This recap of a *USA Today* article is not meant to be definitive on any aspect of Hurricane Katrina, but to give an example of the asking why process. It is a completely different process from asking "who." If Dr. Deming had stated that 100 percent of the problems are caused by the system, the theory would have few if any subscribers. Crime does occur and most if it is not a system problem; individuals own the problem.

A group of school superintendents were asked if they were having a problem with high school cheerleaders. Laughter erupted. They communicated that this was a silly question; of course they were having issues. If any school district is having continual cheerleader problems it is not the fault of the girls and their moms. It is a "why" issue; not a "who" issue. Leaders must ask why, why, why, why, why until they find out why. At the end of the whys will be the root cause of the problem at hand. Society often does not want to deal with the answer. For example, the Raytheon Corporation is attempting to improve middle school mathematics because they hire 4000 engineers a year and are having a supply problem. What if we found out that the key problem with poor mathematics attitudes in middle school was the hatred of math homework? Would society be willing to suspend math homework, in order to keep math enthusiasm up, in order to stop the United State's dependency on foreign engineers? We do not know the answer to the question. What we do know is that the root causes of many problems may be dear to our beliefs. We want homework and we want flood control. It is more fun to sit around and blame, but successful leaders know that blaming is a poor leadership strategy.

Lee's book *Permission to Forget: And Nine Other Root Causes of America's Frustration with Education* essentially is one person's quest into the whys of educational frustration. The title, *Permission to Forget*, also is the first chapter. Essentially, "permission to forget" is a synonym for cramming. When schools give students a system that encourages cramming, they are essentially giving permission to forget. This sounds great to people; let's take away cramming. And then when educators do take away cramming, parents really do need help understanding what problem is being solved. For example, when middle and high schools have a policy for graded exams stating that 70 percent of the exam is to be content from the current course and 30 percent is to be content from prior courses, not everybody is happy. A U.S. history teacher in 11th grade, for example, may be responsible for U.S. history from 1900 to the present day. When he/she changes the exam proportions to 30 percent prior-grade history, it gets people's attention. In this example the 30 percent would be from fifth- and eighth-grade U.S. history. Yes, society wants the students to remember the history and university professors expect the students to enter college remembering the history, but do we really want to take away permission to forget? Is the price worth the benefit?

Again, the point is that leaders have the responsibility to find the root causes of their problems by asking why at least five times. They then have the responsibility to help staff and customers connect the solution to the root cause problem being eliminated. If students do not connect the problems caused by cramming (being unprepared for college, and so on), they will not accept the new course expectations. This is true for all root cause solutions. People must continually make connections between the solution and the problem because they are not immediately connected in the mind.

True, lasting improvement will only occur when leaders ask why enough times to discover the root causes and stop asking only "who" or "why" just long enough to come up with symptoms, not causes. An additional education example of root cause digging may help:

Q: Why are some students struggling so much in school?

A: They did not learn to read very well when they were in kindergarten and first grade.

Q: Any clues as to why they did not learn to read well in kindergarten and first grade?

A: We do not know all of the reasons why, but several students were absent over 50 days in first grade.

Q: Do we know why some were absent so much?

A: Yes, many of the days were because of head lice. Policy is to send children home.

Q: Why did we send them home?; Couldn't we hire somebody for an hour to remove the lice, and send the student back to class?

A: This is not the responsibility of schools; it is the parent's job.

The root cause of the reading struggle for some children is the school's unwillingness to assume the parent's job to take care of the head lice problem. Yes, it is irritating to ask a part-time employee to work an extra 60 to 90 minutes helping a child with head lice. Schools cannot do it all. The problem is that by the time the students are old enough to care for their own hair, the learning-to-read window is over. In this case, the root cause of the reading problem is resentment over having to do the parents' job. Expect to find at the end of the why, why, why, why, why a deep-seated belief that often will be difficult to remove.

E. D. Hirsch has recently written a root cause book on America's reading problem. His analysis of the reading comprehension difficulty students experience, once they learn to decode print, is a lack of background knowledge. He states further that the overbalance upon reading skills instruction is taking away instructional time to build background knowledge. It is in music, art, PE, science, history, and geography that background knowledge is taught. He quotes a study where two groups of students are administered a reading comprehension exam with a baseball story. One group read well, but did not know much about baseball; the second group read poorly but knew a lot about baseball. The second group scored higher on the reading comprehension exam. Hirsch's writing is an excellent example of root cause analysis in education (Hirsch 2006).

Core Values

Visionary leadership. Your school's leaders should set directions and create a student-focused, learning-oriented climate, clear and visible values, and high expectations.

Systems perspective. The Baldrige criteria provide a systems perspective for managing your school and its key processes to achieve results—performance excellence. However, successful management of overall performance requires school-specific synthesis, alignment, and integration.

Baldrige Connection

Describe how your school problem-solves to determine the root causes of concerns or issues. Describe how your school-examination of trends; organizational, academic community, and technology projections; and comparisons, cause-and-effect relationships, and problem-solving models, helps determine root causes, and helps set priorities for resource use.

Guiding Questions

How do you select, collect, align, and integrate data and information, including evidence of student learning, to discover the root causes of educational frustrations?

Adapted from *2005 Education Criteria for Performance Excellence.*

RESOURCES AND READING LIST

Hirsch, E. D., Jr. 2006. *The Knowledge Deficit.* New York: Houghton Mifflin Co.

18

System, Suboptimization, and Non-Systems: The Left Hand and the Right Hand

OVERVIEW

Most people have experienced non-systems; we know when the left hand does not know what the right hand is doing. Serious examples of non-system thinking are an elementary school that reads *Charlotte's Web* five years in a row or a curriculum that teaches about Christopher Columbus in the first, third, fifth, eighth, and 10th grades. It happens in universities when every professor is allowed to have his/her own rules for term papers. It inadvertently occurs in business when the transmission engineers are in competition with the engine engineers for a bonus. A non-system is present when everybody is working individually, even if doing their best work.

Every organization has seemingly an infinite number of different pieces to put together. Customers expect that somebody somewhere is coordinating all of these efforts. Most of us have experienced entering our account number into a touch-tone phone. We must enter the account number so we can talk to a real person. We comply. We wait. We listen to ads and music. After several more computers, the real person comes who asks for the account number. We respond, "It was just entered into your computer." The real person says, "That was for the computer (left hand); I am a real person (right hand) and do not have access to the computer." We relate this experience because it is a real struggle to get all aspects of a system to function smoothly. Only the leader, with constant help, can accomplish smoothness—a system that functions the way customers desire.

Another example of a non-system is school grading policies. In the authors' two-day seminars, teachers are asked to answer this question: "If a student in your classroom earns an A on all exams and an A on all of the projects and long-term assignments, but refuses to hand in short-term, daily homework, what is the highest grade this student can earn in your classroom?" The answers are A, B, C, D, F; all five come from the same faculty. Teachers absolutely do not agree on the answer to the question. This is a non-system that only the principal, as leader, can fix with great assistance from the staff.

Suboptimization occurs when one aspect of an organization wins over another aspect of the organization. Athletic teams want fans to buy tickets. Some have contracted with one organization to sell tickets online and another organization to sell tickets by phone. Suppose you go online to buy tickets but later decide you'd rather purchase by phone. In some instances you would be hard-pressed to find the phone number on the Web site. Why? The Web site contract holders do not make a commission on phone purchases. This is suboptimization; one aspect of an organization wins at the expense of another part. Each aspect is attempting to win at the expense of another aspect.

Deming (1986) told the classic story of the head of engines at a major automobile manufacturer refusing to save $50 per car because it would decrease his bonus. An idea proposed by an employee would have increased the cost of engines by $20 and decreased the cost of transmissions by $70. Since the head of engines knew his bonus was based on engine costs, not on total car costs, he said no to the cost-saving idea. The CEO of the company had set up the bonus structure to suboptimize the company. According to Heylighen, et al. (1999), generally the outcome of a system as a whole cannot be optimized by simply optimizing the outcome of any subsystem. They go on to point out that this intrinsic difficulty may cause the exhaustion of shared resources because of competition between subsystems.

When a system is optimized, the left hand and right hand know what each other are doing and everybody is working for the good of the company. All can win. We usually call this a "well-oiled" system.

The problem with creating a system that functions well is that it is much easier to see the non-system failing than to create a system that works. For example, a school superintendent might be required to give the same exact information to four different departments in the state capitol in the same week. This same frustrated school superintendent does not know that his very own school secretaries are giving four different people in his/her own central office the same exact information in the same week.

Think about the current collection of human services—education, health, and welfare—for America's youth and their families. It is just that, a "collection" of services, not a unified system. This is not a new problem; the National Association of State Boards of Education provides an example:

At the federal level alone, over $10 billion in 27 separate programs support early childhood activities (Sugarman 1991). Early childhood programs may be funded through the Department of Education via Chapter 1, Even Start, PL 99-457, as well as from the Department of Health and Human Services through Head Start, the Child Care and Development Block Grant Program, the Social Service Block Grant Program, and a number of work-related child care programs. Parents also receive support from the Internal Revenue Service via the child care tax credit. This proliferation of programs is mirrored and extended at the state level, resulting in a variety of serious problems for local government, for program providers, and most seriously for families and children (NASBE 1991, 22).

One of the major reasons leaders must listen, listen, and listen some more is that employees often do not see the system disconnects. It is the customers who see that the "left hand" does not know what the "right hand" is doing. The five teachers reading *Charlottes's Web* five years in a row do not know this is occurring; the parents and students know, however.

Readers of this book are customers of many organizations. Think how many times you have walked out of a business determined to never return. You have information in your head the leader of the organization should have, but the leader will probably never find out. As leader of your organization it is important that you find out as much as you can about these disconnects so that the system, as a whole, operates efficiently.

Core Values

Systems perspective. Operations are characterized by processes that are repeatable and regularly evaluated for change and improvement in collaboration with other affected units. Efficiencies across units are sought and achieved through analysis, innovation, and sharing. Processes and measures track progress on key strategic and operational goals.

Baldrige Connection

Describe how your faculty and staff are organized into formal or informal units to accomplish your mission and your strategic objectives, how job responsibilities are managed, and your processes for compensation, faculty and staff performance management, recognition, communication, hiring, and succession planning.

Continued

Continued

Describe the "leadership system"; this refers to how leadership is exercised, formally and informally, throughout the organization—the basis for and the way that key decisions are made, communicated, and carried out. It includes structures and mechanisms for decision making, selection and development of senior leaders, administrators, department heads, and faculty leaders, and reinforcement of values, ethical behavior, directions, and performance expectations.

Guiding Questions

What are the systematic processes that make up the system and its subsystems? For example, a systematic process might describe the communication methods used by all senior leaders to deliver performance expectations on a regular basis to all faculty and staff, the measures used to assess the effectiveness of the methods, and the tools and techniques used to evaluate and improve the communication methods. In other words, approaches are systematic if they build-in the opportunity for evaluation, improvement, and sharing, thereby permitting a gain in maturity

Adapted from *2005 Education Criteria for Performance Excellence.*

RESOURCES AND READING LIST

Barker, Joel Arthur. 1992. *Future Edge: Discovering the New Paradigms of Success.* New York: William Morrow and Co.

Brown, John Seely. 1988. *Seeing Differently: Insights on Innovation.* Boston: Harvard Business Review.

Burrus, Daniel, with Roger Gittines. 1993. *Technotrends: How to Use Technology to Go beyond your Competition.* New York: HarperBusiness.

Checkland, Peter B. 1999. *Systems Thinking, Systems Practice.* Chichester, England: John Wiley & Sons.

Deming, W. Edwards. 1986. *Out of the Crisis.* Cambridge, MA: MIT Center for Advanced Engineering Study.

———. 1994. *The New Economics for Industry, Government, Education,* 2nd ed. Cambridge, MA: MIT Center for Advanced Engineering Study.

Drucker, Peter. 1985. *Innovation and Entrepreneurship.* New York: HarperCollins.

Hamel, Gary. 2000. *Leading the Revolution.* Boston: Harvard Business School Press.

Heylighen, Francis, Johan Bollen, and Alexander Riegler, eds. 1999. *The Evolution of Complexity.* Dordrecht: Kluwer Academic.

Hirshberg, Jerry. 1998. *The Creative Priority: Driving Innovative Business in the Real World.* New York: HarperCollins.

Jackson, Michael C. 2000. *Systems Approaches to Management.* New York: Kluwer/Plenum.

Kelley, Tom, with Jonathan Littman. 2001. *The Art of Innovation: Lessons in Creativity from IDEO, America's Leading Design Firm.* New York: Random House.

Maani, Kambiz E., and Robert Y. Cavana. 2000. *Systems Thinking and Modelling.* New Zealand: Pearson Education.

Rodin, Robert. 1999. *Free, Perfect, and Now: Connecting to the Three Insatiable Customer Demands: A CEO's True Story.* New York: Simon & Schuster.

Senge, Peter. 1990. *The Fifth Discipline: The Art and Practice of the Learning Organization.* New York: Doubleday.

19

Customers: We All Have Them

OVERVIEW

All organizations have customers. Not all organizations use the word customer; nevertheless they all have customers. Hospitals have customers called patients, churches have customers called parishioners, teams have customers called fans, and schools have customers called students. We never expect professional sports to stop using the term fan and replace it with customer and we never expect education to drop the word student for the word customer. Customer, however, is the generic term that is used so that all professions can have dialog about common issues.

Beyond the obvious—an organization with no customers goes out of business—what is the value of studying customers? The value is the insight they provide. Customers see things that employees will never see. Employees need the insights of customers in order to do their best. Everyone reading this book is a worker with customers and is also a customer of other workers. When we are customers we have valuable insights that need to be shared. When we are the worker we need to have proactive ways to glean the customers' insights.

It has often been repeated that an "open door" policy is the best. This is not true. On a continuum from worst communication to best communication, open door is in the middle. At the left side of the communication continuum is the person with the worst communication skills; this person may listen to his/her friends. In the middle of the continuum is the open door. The open door policy states that if you will take the initiative to speak to me, my door is open. However, if you do not take the initiative, I will never know your thoughts. The communication responsibility rests on the customer, not on the worker. At the far right side of the continuum is the worker who proactively seeks input from customers. This person does not wait for the customer to offer suggestions, but asks ahead of time.

Let's use a minister as an example. The worst minister communicators can never be found during the week. They hide and only a few friends know how to talk with them. The next level of minister communicator is always available to talk. The church secretary has authority to establish appointments and if you call for an appointment it is guaranteed that you'll meet. At the highest level of minister communication is the one that is continually asking members of the congregation, "What went well in our church this past month and what could we do to make next month better?" This minister thinks, "I haven't spoken one on one with a certain person for a couple of months; I need to check in on him/her."

In education, there is debate over who is the customer. The truth of the matter is that education has many customers, but the key customer is the student. It is essential that educators learn from the students. The students have observations of which adults are oblivious. Teachers are often much like the mid-level minister described above: they will drop everything to deal with a needy student, but have not been shown how to work at the highest level of communication. Listening to students is at the summit of communication.

Why should one listen to students? Since everyone reading this book is a customer of various organizations, everyone knows they have suggestions regarding how a particular business could better meet their needs. We do not want to become the banker, but we know how the bank could better meet our needs. The same is true for students. They have ideas on how we, as educators, could better meet their needs. And the truth of the matter is that they have ideas that will help future students.

Darren Overton, principal of Pine Island Middle School, improved his school's discipline by listening to troublemakers. He called into his office a group of 17 students. These students were the ones with two or more discipline referrals during the first three quarters of the school year. He gave them the task of helping him make the school better. They talked for 90 minutes, giving suggestions. Darren made some schoolwide changes based on the advice of the troublemakers. Think about it: who is the customer of principal punishments? It is a small group of students. These customers have a lot of insight not shared by the majority of the student body. They can help us a lot.

Surveys are a part of a customer focus. Schools send out surveys to parents and attempt to make decisions based on the feedback. This is probably a waste of time. Why? Because the 10 percent return rate often does not give the best advice. What is the best way to listen to parent-customers? It is probably better to randomly select a small sample of parents and interview them on the phone. This way the principal will have accurate information from the whole set of parents. If, on the other hand, a school has figured out a way to have a 90 percent return rate on questionnaires, they should continue with questionnaires.

Customer satisfaction is clearly one of the best reasons for any system to celebrate all-time-bests. An example of a message that could be sent out from the principal is:

"As readers know, we survey 30 parents, randomly selected, each quarter. These parents are asked to rate the school experience of one child, on a scale of 1 through 5, in a dozen aspects of the school experience. Each quarter we average the responses. This quarter the average of all 460 questions was 4.23. This tops our prior all-time-best of 4.18. Thanks to all members of our staff."

Core Values

Valuing faculty, staff, and partners by leadership who is not only dependent on but committed to the knowledge, skills, innovative creativity, and motivation of its workforce.

Agility with an explicit focus on faster and more flexible responses to needs of students and stakeholders.

Baldrige Connection

Students are the key customers of education schools, but there may be multiple stakeholders, for example, parents, employers, other schools, and communities.

Describe how your school determines requirements, expectations, and preferences of students, stakeholders, and markets to ensure the continuing relevance of your educational programs, offerings, and services, to develop new opportunities, and to create an overall climate conducive to learning and development for all students.

Continued

Continued

Guiding Questions

How do you identify your current customer base, that is, the student and market segments your educational programs address? How do you determine which student and market segments to pursue for current and future educational programs, offerings, and services? How do you include customers (students) currently served by other education providers and other potential students and markets in this determination? How do you listen and learn to determine customers' (students' and stakeholders') key requirements and changing expectations (including educational program, offering, and service features) and their relative importance to these customers' decisions related to enrollment?

Adapted from *2005 Education Criteria for Performance Excellence.*

20

School Safety: A Never-Ending Challenge

OVERVIEW

School safety is possibly the biggest headline grabber of the last decade. According to *Early Warning, Timely Response: A Guide to Safe Schools* (1997), less than one percent of violent deaths occur at school, and Merrow (2004) states that students have only a one in six million chance of being shot at school. However, the perception is that our schools are potentially dangerous places. Safety is a very important issue regardless of the actual statistics. Fear of violence or bullying creates stress, and according to Delpit (as cited in Merrow), learning shuts down under such conditions. It is the job of the principal to establish and enforce policies that make their students and staff feel safe so that learning may happen.

There are three kinds of safety that a principal must keep in mind: physical, emotional, and intellectual. Most people focus on physical safety. Some schools try to do this through metal detectors, video cameras, and zero tolerance policies, but Colgan (2005) suggests that schools confront the issue of safety with collaboration and communication. This involves having frequent staff and student reviews of school behavior expectations, peer mediation, talking about safety issues to improve the current system, and training for handling everyday issues and crises alike.

A school leader should also provide for emotional and intellectual safety. Emotional safety is most commonly violated by bullying and teasing. Although schools cannot eliminate bullying and teasing altogether, they can intervene to decrease their frequency. Creating an alliance with students to police these negative behaviors can result in a more welcoming atmosphere. Intellectual safety provides students with the opportunity to take risks and ask probing questions without the fear of being made fun of. "An intellectually safe school values ideas and explorations" (Merrow, 28). An eighth grader was asked, "Do you learn more from teachers you like or teachers you do not like?" She replied, "We learn a lot more from teachers we like." "Why?" the questioning continued. "We learn more from teachers we like, because, the teachers we do not like, we never ask them questions." Why do students not ask questions of teachers they do not like? The answer is they do not feel intellectually safe; they never know if they will be embarrassed, ridiculed, or given a roll of the eyes.

IMPLEMENTATION STEPS

The following steps are adapted from Merrow (2004) and suggest ways to help students cope with difficult situations:

1. Let students express how they feel

2. Model tolerance and empathy

3. Comfort students by showing them that you care through listening and giving them heightened attention

4. Answer their questions honestly

Take the following steps if you believe your school or district has gangs:

School district leaders should:

- Do everything possible to create a safe campus

- Provide students with an anonymous reporting system

- Create an emergency response plan and teach it to all staff members

- Work with the local emergency service providers to encourage immediate assistance during a school crisis or emergency

- Have someone designated to be in charge during an emergency if you are absent or incapacitated

- Document any concern or action associated with school safety

- Make monitoring safety and security a priority for the district's maintenance department

- Practice strategic supervision

Principals should:

- Adopt a "zero tolerance" policy toward gang activity
- Establish the school as neutral ground
- Distinguish between deviant and criminal acts
- Have knowledge of community resources
- Train school personnel in how to identify and handle gang members
- Mediate student conflicts

Teachers should:

- Be consistent and fair
- Teach students how to problem-solve and make good decisions
- Teach about the rights and responsibilities of others
- Communicate with and involve parents

Bullying Prevention Tips

Students: (Post for students to see)

- Do not retaliate or get angry
- Say nothing and walk away
- Tell a teacher, counselor, or principal
- Tell your parents
- Try to avoid being alone
- Avoid unsupervised areas of school
- Take a different route to and from school
- Do not bring expensive items to school

Parents: (Send home to parents)

- Do not tell your child to fight or hit back
- Ask your child to share problems with you
- Help your child to develop new friendships

- Maintain contact with your child's school
- Keep a detailed record of bullying episodes and communication with the school
- Encourage your child to participate in sports or physical activity
- Praise and encourage your child

Principals:

- Use students' surveys to determine if there is a bullying problem
- Create a bullying prevention committee
- Establish an anti-bullying plan
- Get parents involved in planning
- Establish classroom rules against bullying
- Create positive and negative consequences vis-à-vis bullying
- Speak with bullies, tell them it is unacceptable behavior and they must stop
- Talk with victims of bullying

TOOLS

A Parent's Quick Reference Card: Recognizing and Preventing Gang Involvement

Produced by the Office of Community Oriented Policing Services, United States Department of Justice, this reference card lists warning signs indicating that a child may be involved in a gang and actions parents can take to prevent gang involvement. Parents are encouraged to familiarize themselves with local gang symbols, seek help early, and consider contacting school officials, local law enforcement, faith leaders, and community organizations for additional assistance.

Crisis Management Plan

Another necessary component of school safety is a Crisis Management Plan. According to Schonefeld, Lichtenstein, Kline-Pruett, and Speese-Linehan (2002):

1. Crisis situations are inevitable in a school setting.

2. Crisis involves people and their personal reactions to the situation. It is not the situation, but the reaction to the situation that characterizes crisis.

A crisis can take many forms including, but not limited to, a fire, tornado, bomb threat, accident or death of a student or staff member, school intruder, or student violence. With this in mind, it is essential that the school have a plan in place to manage a crisis when it occurs.

Since people react differently to crisis, a well-designed plan that has been practiced and is reviewed on a regular basis can help in a major way to alleviate some of the negative reactions that can occur in a crisis. The plan should be developed by a committee made up of school stakeholders. While information can be gleaned from crisis plans of other sites, it is important that the team develop a plan specific to their site. This plan should be a part of the school items provided to each teacher and should be addressed in the substitute teacher plan. The book by Schoenfield, et al. is an excellent resource for devising a crisis plan.

Not only should there be a plan, but elements of the plan should be practiced regularly. This goes beyond the fire drill to include other potential elements of crisis. Teachers and staff also should be provided training concerning the best steps in a crisis situation and should be provided opportunities to role-play responses.

While managing a building aimed at ensuring physical, emotional, and intellectual safety, and developing and practicing a crisis management plan can help reduce the safety problems of a school, it is important to realize that 100 percent safety is probably an impossible goal. However, these safeguards can reduce the safety stress sometimes associated with schools and allow all to focus on the real issue—improving all students' performance.

Core Values

Social responsibility. A school's leaders should stress responsibilities to the public, ethical behavior, protection of public health, safety, and the environment, and the need to practice good citizenship.

Baldrige Connection

Describe how planning anticipates adverse impacts to school safety that might arise in facilities management, laboratory operations, and

---

Continued

Continued

transportation. Describe how your school prevents problems, provides for a forthright response if problems occur, and makes available information and support needed to maintain public safety and confidence.

Guiding Questions

What are your key compliance processes, measures, and goals for achieving and surpassing safety requirements? What is your school's safe school plan?

Adapted from *2005 Education Criteria for Performance Excellence.*

RESOURCES AND READING LIST

Brunner, June, and Dennis Lewis. 2005. "A Safe School's Top 10 Needs." [Electronic version]. *Education Digest* 71, no. 1: 21–24.

Colgan, Craig. March 2003. "The New Look of School Safety." *American School Board Journal* 192. http://www.nsba.org/site/doc.asp?TRACKID =&vid=2&CID=1234&DID=35711.

Davis, Stan, and Julia Lewis. 2005. *Schools Where Everyone Belongs: Practical Strategies for Reducing Bullying.* Champaign, IL: Research Press.

Dwyer, Kevin, David Osher, and Cynthia Warger. 1998. *Early Warning, Timely Response: A Guide to Safe Schools: The Referenced Edition.* Washington, DC: American Institutes for Research.

McGrath, Mary Jo. 2007. *School Bullying: Tools for Avoiding Harm and Liability.* Thousand Oaks, CA: Corwin Press.

Merrow, John. 2004. "Safety and Excellence." [Electronic version]. *Educational Horizons.* 83, no. 1: 19–32.

Schonefeld, David J., Robert Lichtenstein, Marsha Kline-Pruett, and Dee Speese-Linehan. 2002. *How to Prepare for and Respond to a Crisis.* Baltimore, MD: Association for Supervision and Curriculum Development.

Ubben, Gerald C., Larry W. Hughes, and Cynthia J. Norris. 2004. *The Principal: Creative Leadership for Excellence in Schools.* Boston: Pearson Education.

LINKS

Gang prevention/education: http://www.helpinggangyouth.com

National youth violence prevention: http://www.safeyouth.org/scripts/teens.asp

Students Against Violence Everywhere (S.A.V.E.): www.nationalsave.org/index.php

Office of Safe and Drug-Free Schools: http://www.ed.gov/about/offices/list/osdfs/index.html

Part III

Using the Fundamentals to Achieve Excellence

21

Cooperation and Competition: Fundamental Understandings

OVERVIEW

Cooperation is a method. Competition is a method. Homework is a method. Although homework is not the topic of this chapter, mentioning it helps make the point regarding method. The aim in schools is learning, and homework is a method of accomplishing the learning for many students. Completed homework is not the goal; learning is the goal. Cooperation and competition are also methods, not goals. Both can be used to increase learning.

In December 2005, we heard one of the 50 state school superintendents advocate a return to spelling bees since competition is what makes America great. It seems the advocating of spelling bees, in this case, is not for the improvement of spelling. Instead, the competition involved in the spelling bee is viewed as a subject to be learned. A more reasoned statement might be, "We need to improve spelling in our state, and I would like some school districts to consider testing whether or not spelling test results will increase with spelling bees."

There are two types of competition: internal and external. With internal competition, employees and team members are competitors. The leader believes the company will make more money if the employees compete with each other. The view is that internal competition is the best method to make the company externally competitive. The opposite view is held by others, who believe that employees should cooperate with each other. Internal cooperation is viewed as the best way to be externally competitive.

In education, any discussion regarding competition must be predicated by the question, "What type of competition are you suggesting—external or internal?" The state superintendent mentioned earlier clearly believes that internal competition among students is the best way for her state to be externally competitive with other states.

Cooperation in education is often discussed with such passion that one might conclude cooperative learning is a subject; it is not. Both cooperation and competition are methods used to increase learning. When cooperation and competition are discussed, there is often a significant lack of background knowledge to inform the discussion. The benefits society gains from cooperation and the two types of competition often are not understood or distinguished.

There are many examples of interstate cooperation that make life easier. No matter which state one travels to, the electrical outlets are the same. Rules for sports are the same in all states. Basic driving rules are consistent from state to state. Even the connectors for LCD projectors have been standardized so all laptops can be connected no matter the brand of computer or projector. The benefit of cooperation in society would make a good United States social studies lesson. Some cooperation occurs because of business agreements and some occurs because legislators cooperated. Life would be ridiculously complex if every state had different electrical outlets, different rules for baseball, and disagreement regarding which side of the road one drives on. Students should not take for granted the benefits of cooperation.

Our belief is that internal cooperation in business, sports, and education is necessary to be the most competitive externally. Businesspeople, athletes, and students need to cooperate with each other in order to learn the most. However, we recognize that without the types of data described in Chapter 12 on process data, students do not know if their cooperation is working.

Business authors Pfeffer and Sutton (*The Knowing–Doing Gap*) entitle their chapter on competition, "When Internal Competition Turns Friends into Enemies." In the midst of their very insightful chapter on the destructive nature of internal competition, they wrote, "No manager wanted to admit that he or she had anything to learn from anyone else because they were in competition with each other." A key point they make is, "Trying to do well and trying to beat others are two different things."

So, can internal competition ever be good? Pfeffer and Sutton say yes, in spite of their chapter title. "Competition is more useful under conditions of less interdependence and for activities that do not require much learning because the skills are already well honed."

Since the very purpose of schools is learning, it is highly unlikely that internal competition will be helpful. This flies in the face of such practices as spelling bees, limiting valedictorians to one per high school, bell-curve grading policies, and any other event with winners and losers. One cannot deny that the excitement of competition to win the science fair has some motivational benefits. The problem comes after the science fair when almost all the students are demotivated in science. The students fully understand that second place is "loser number one."

So, can competition in schools ever be helpful? Yes. It is helpful in anything that is a game. This includes sports and other activities that are academic. Games are for fun and competitive games are fun. Another good use of competition is to encourage students to outperform prior groups of students. When the fourth-graders, all together, are attempting to outperform last year's fourth graders, competition can be good.

Education is not a game; it is serious business. Every country needs as many successful, well-educated people as possible. United States citizens need to decide who is internal and who is external. If we are to cooperate internally in order to be more competitive externally, then who is internal? By logging onto the National Assessment of Educational Progress (NAEP) Web site (http://nces.ed.gov/nationsreportcard/nrc/reading_math_2005/s0023.asp?printver=), one can view a map of the United States. A click on a state sets the color of the state to blue. Then all other states are color coded depending on how they scored compared to the first-clicked state. What this communicates is that states are competitors in education. Should this be? Our view is that states should not be competitors. It does no good for our country to always have loser states. People move from state to state; we are a nation. Therefore, a better view of education would be to have states cooperate with each other in order to be more internationally competitive.

We realize that the United States has a long way to go in this regard. We also realize that readers of this book cannot change the culture in regard to state-to-state competition. However, readers of this book can determine to have internal cooperation in their sphere of influence. Superintendents can establish a culture of cooperation between schools or they can establish a culture in which schools within a school district are competitors. Principals have the same power in their schools, as do teachers in their classrooms.

The power of internal cooperation rarely has been understood or experienced in schools. With internal cooperation, students in classes, grade levels, and departments are working together to score higher than ever before. A simple example is reading fluency. If a school has 100 second-graders, and the expectation is that second-graders read 100 words per minute on fluency assessments, then all the second graders together are attempting to read 10,000 words in a minute. The principal graphs the combined results from the monthly assessments and posts them in the hallway or foyer of the school. This provides the principal ample opportunity to help all students to increase.

The normal process in schools is internal competition. A star is made for each student and is placed in the hallway. The students' stars are placed according to fluency rates. The false notion is that a student will be motivated by having his/her star at the far left and will work hard to move it to the right side. False thinking. The student is demotivated by everyone seeing his/her star on the losing side. However, when there is only the total for the whole grade level in the hallway, everyone gets to contribute to the success of the grade level. All students want to help each other so that all can increase. If there is a need to add competition, then see if this year's second-graders can outperform last year's second graders.

As with all of the elements discussed in this book, cooperation and competition should be used to help students continually improve their performance. The correct use of these tools or methods can foster a climate of learning. That is the final goal.

Core Values

Agility with an explicit focus on faster and more flexible responses to needs of students and stakeholders.

Focus on the future that takes into account both short-term and longer-term factors that affect the school.

Baldrige Connection

Describe your school's competitive environment, your key strategic challenges, and your system for performance improvement. These challenges might include the anticipation of and adjustment for your operational costs, an expanding or decreasing student population, a decreasing local and state tax base or educational appropriation, changing demographics and competition, including charter schools, diminishing student persistence, the introduction of new or substitute programs, services, or offerings, possibly based on a disruptive technology, and state and federal mandates.

Guiding Questions

How do you ensure that strategic planning addresses your school's strengths, weaknesses, opportunities, and threats and early indications of educational reform and major shifts in technology, student and community demographics, markets, competition, or the regulatory environment. What initiatives are in place or available to promote greater labor–management cooperation, such as union partnerships?

Adapted from *2005 Education Criteria for Performance Excellence.*

RESOURCES AND READING LIST

Pfeffer, Jeffrey, and Robert I. Sutton. 2000. *The Knowing–Doing Gap: How Smart Companies Turn Knowledge into Action.* Boston: Harvard Business School Press.

22

Measuring for Results: The Summative Data at Year's End

OVERVIEW

There are several purposes for collecting results data. None of the purposes are to determine if one school, district, or state outperformed another school, district, or state. This lack of understanding may well be the major reason congress passed the No Child Left Behind legislation. If a particular school outperformed neighboring schools, then it was determined that the school was okay. The problem is that all was not okay. A portion of the students were not doing well. If the school at the top of the heap had five of its 150 first-graders who did not learn to read and other schools in the city had from 10 to 50 of their first-graders struggling with reading, then the top school was praised and left alone. All of this misunderstanding comes from inappropriate use of results data.

So, if the purpose of collecting results data is not to see who won the contest, what are the purposes? The purposes are twofold: (1) did we improve and (2) what insights can we gain from this test data to help us improve for next year? Simply put, improvement can and should be measured continuously. Without the metrics of results data one could not identify the all-time-bests. Absent this data, a culture of continuous improvement will not be created.

The responsibility of the leader is to define improvement. It means fewer students experiencing failure and more students experiencing success. This means that for each educational endeavor there must be agreement on what constitutes success and what constitutes failure. Then for each measured aspect of schooling, the leader's job is to determine if improvement occurred. In writing, this could be answering the question, "Did we have more students writing at level 3 and 4 on the state writing exam (1–4 scale) and fewer students writing at level 1?" If so, we improved in writing. For attendance, "Did we have more students who met our criteria for success (>95 percent attendance, for example) and fewer students who met our criteria for failure in attendance (<85 percent attendance, for example)." And so on.

The radar chart (Chapter 3) is the most efficient way of displaying all of this data on two sheets of paper: one radar chart for success and one for failure. When there is a high degree of success, the radar chart is easy to read because all the dots and lines are at the outer edge of the chart. When there is almost no failure, the failure radar chart cannot be effectively read because all of the dots and lines are clumped at the zero. This is good. We have observed radar charts tracking 25 or more attributes of schooling. One such radar chart was a mess around the zero, with one point sticking way out. This graphic provided a dramatic way for the leader to communicate an opportunity for improvement.

TOOLS

The rest of this chapter is about utilizing the results data to gain insight into how to improve for the next year. The tools are in order of the details they provide. First are the most global pictures and gradually the graphs open up more and more insight.

One-Line Run Chart

This graph plots one line for the whole school or whole school district. It is the percent of tests where the student scored proficient or advanced. This graph puts all subjects and grade levels together into one line. It answers the "Chamber of Commerce" question: "Did we improve—yes or no?" Figure 22.1 is a depiction of the results of our continuous improvement project at Miami, Arizona, showing the percentage of K–8 students meeting or exceeding state standards as measured by the AIMS test.

Success and Failure Run Chart

This run chart is the one-line run chart with one more line added: the failure line. This graph answers the "Did we improve" question with more detail in that improvement is defined as both an increase in success and a decrease in failure. The failure line is added, making this a two-line graph. Often there is some information left out on this graph: not all exams are

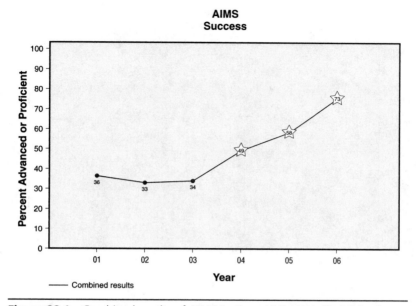

Figure 22.1 Combined results of AIMS testing at Miami Unified School District, Arizona.

represented. For example, if a school receives test results in student writing on a 1–4 scale, it is reasonable to assign level 1 papers to the failure line and level 3–4 papers to the success line, thus leaving the level 2 papers ungraphed. Schools also have done this with percentile information, where below the 25th percentile is designated as failure and the 50th percentile and above as success. The reason for this separation is that the tests are not perfect and their standard error of measurement can vary significantly. Lee County, Florida, gave their students a nationally normed reading test and corrected the results with their 1 to 5 scale state exam. Level 1 students averaged at the 30th percentile, level 2 at the 60th percentile, and level 3 at the 66th percentile. This data supports the advice to count levels 3, 4, 5 in Florida as success and level 1 as failure. Level 2 is left out of this graph. One would not want to say that a student at the 50th percentile is successful and a student at the 49th percentile is in need of significant help. However, when students score below the 25th percentile, the test almost always accurately predicts the lack of these students' success or content area mastery, which means there is a need for additional assistance to reduce this failure. Figure 22.2 is a comparison of the increasing success to the decreasing failure at MUSD.

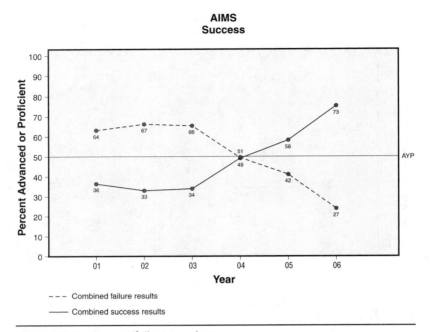

Figure 22.2 Success/failure run chart.

The Bottom Line

This is not a graph but consists of reading other graphs to determine a simple yes or no for each measure of graduating students. By comparing this year's annual graphs to previous years' annual graphs, one can answer the query: Did the school graduate the best-prepared students ever?

a. In language arts?   Yes or No

b. In mathematics?   Yes or No

c. In history/social science?   Yes or No

d. In science?   Yes or No

e. In the arts?   Yes or No

By comparing the 2005–2006 scores in reading, math, and writing, one can clearly see that the school has better prepared this year's students than at any time in the past (Figure 22.3).

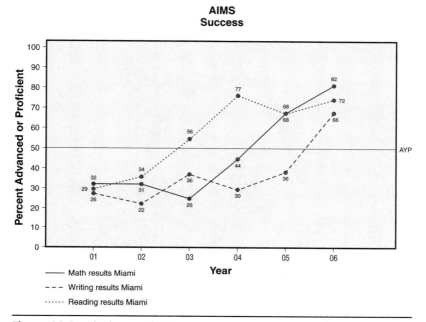

AIMS
Success

——— Math results Miami
– – – Writing results Miami
······ Reading results Miami

Figure 22.3 The bottom line comparison graph.

Radar Chart

Some people outside the organization and all within an organization need more information than is supplied by the first three graphs. They want specifics. What about third-grade math, for example? It is not enough to know generally. Many in the public do not want all of the detail provided by the radar chart; most within an organization do want it. Figure 22.4 is an example of a radar chart.

Scatter Diagram

This chart plots a dot for each entity, each time data is gathered. The graph in this chapter is a scatter diagram for fourth-grade math results from the National Assessment of Educational Progress. The y-axis is the scale from NAEP and the x-axis represents the years the assessment has been given. Each dot is a state. (A circle represents 10 states.) The scatter diagram can be used for classrooms, as described in *Improving Student Learning,* for schools, districts, or states. If it were to be for states, then each dot would be a school. The KnowledgePower legend uses a box for 100 schools and an

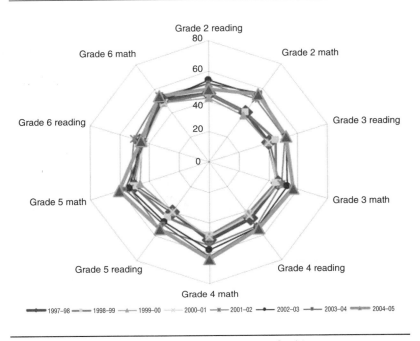

Figure 22.4   A radar chart depicting seven years of achievement.

X for 1000 schools. The advantage of the scatter diagram is that it allows the viewer to gain a much more complete picture of an entity. For example, on the NAEP graph (Figure 22.5) one can see that all states are increasing their students' knowledge of math in fourth grade.

Correlation Chart

This graph informs people regarding the correlation of two variables. In the context of this book, the two variables are process data and results data. Leaders need to know if the processes they are leading correlate to the final results. Do student scores on process data match student scores on results data? A visual comparison of the results on the Indiana state test (ISTEP) and the process data from the same students shows an almost perfect correlation between process and results data (see Figure 22.6). The two students at the lower left of the graph scored poorly on both the process and results assessments. The student at the top right scored very well on both process and results. However, the correlation is not perfect. Four students, in the lower middle of the graph (circled) should have scored higher on the state assessment.

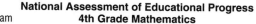

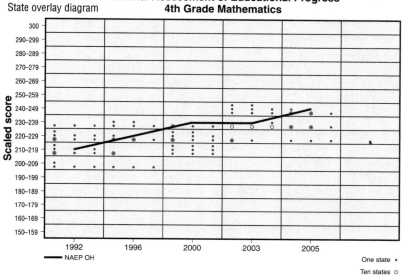

Figure 22.5 National Assessment of Educational Progress.

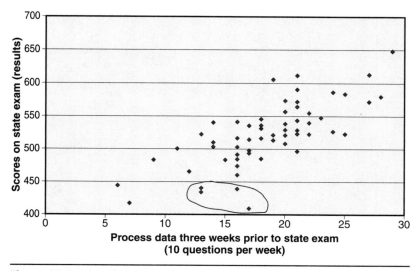

Figure 22.6 Correlation chart.

This graph was produced with Excel—XY Scatter. We prefer to call this a correlation chart. The actual correlation coefficient is .74.

Disaggregation

In today's educational lexicon, one hears the word disaggregation so often it would seem that it is the place to start. However, disaggregation is not the place to start. The first responsibility of school leaders is for everybody to improve. Next come the questions, "Are we closing achievement gaps?" and "What insight can we gain from studying subsets of students?" One middle school, for example, disaggregated math process results according to gender and then according to gender and whether or not the students were on free or reduced lunch. The gender graphs for grades 6, 7, and 8 showed the boys and girls tied in grades 6 and 7, but the boys ahead of the girls in grade 8. When income level was added, boys and girls not on free lunch were tied at the top in grade 8, then came boys on free lunch, and then came girls on free lunch. Through disaggregation, they were able to understand that, at their school, gender was not an issue in math unless poverty was present. This is insight that can assist leaders in improving schooling. See Figure 22.7.

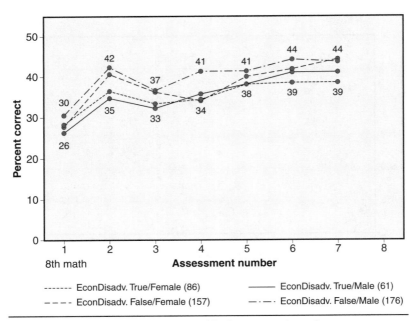

Figure 22.7   Run chart disaggregated by income and gender.

Item Analysis

The Pareto chart is the most sophisticated instrument for analyzing results, by item or strand, from standardized exams. Almost every time we have helped school leaders create Pareto charts from their results data, the administrators said, "Oops, we gave the teachers the wrong advice on what to emphasize next year." The directions for making a Pareto chart with Excel are in the following sidebar. The Pareto chart in Figure 22.8 was developed using these instructions. Table 22.1 shows the data used to construct the chart. QI macros also can be purchased to create more sophisticated Pareto charts.

Steps for Creating a Pareto Chart

In Excel, set up a spreadsheet such that the first column contains the descriptions or definitions of your data, the second column contains categories of the data, the third column contains, percentages of each category, the fourth column cumulative percentages of each category, the fifth column number of occurrences per category, and the sixth column cumulative number of incidences.

1. Identify all possible categories.

2. Label columns.

3. List data in number column.

4. Create total of number column (N) using formula: =sum(E3:E27).

5. If the data is not sorted from high to low, then sort the data from the highest percentage to the lowest. The sequence for sorting is: "Data," "Sort," "Percent," "Descending."

6. In percent column compute % using this formula: Cell # of row and column divided by total of data (N) formula: =C3/C26 in this example.

7. In cumulative percent column compute running total % using this formula: first cell = corresponding first cell # in percent column =C3, second cell = previous cell plus second corresponding cell =D3+C4; repeat for each cell.

8. Repeat Step 7 for the cumulative numbers column.

9. Next, highlight "Categories," "Percent," and "Cumulative Percent" columns. Go to Chart Wizard, select "Custom Types" and select "Line-Columns."

10. Create axis titles and name chart; create as a new sheet in the workbook.

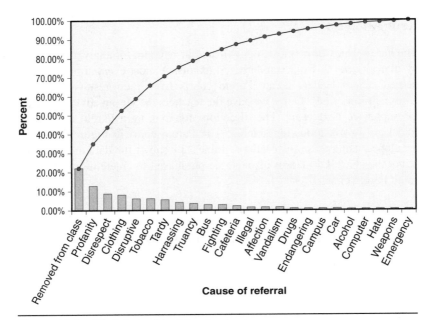

Figure 22.8   Discipline referral Pareto chart.

Control Chart

The control chart is designed to separate special from common variation. What data is truly special (bad or good)? Ranking does not provide this information. The fact that a school is in first place does not make it special. The fact that a school is in last place does not make it special. Special means it is significantly different from other schools. The control chart mathematically separates special variation from common variation. One way to understand this better is with eighth-graders' reading levels. A student in eighth grade reading like an average seventh- or ninth-grader does not possess special reading ability. This variation is common. On the other hand, a student reading like an average fourth-grader is special, as is the student reading like an average 12th-grader. The control chart helps us separate out all this variation.

Cohort Analysis

Sometimes educators go to conferences and hear speakers say that one cannot compare third-graders to third-graders. They go on to say that the only reliable data are cohort data that follow the students from second to

Table 22.1 School discipline referral data used to construct Pareto chart.

Description	Category	Percent	Cumulative Percent	Number	Cumulative Numbers
Removed, sent out of class to the office for any reason.	Removed	22%	22%	225	225
Saying or writing for others to see obscene, *profane* language.	Profanity	13%	35%	134	359
Showing *disrespect* toward a staff member.	Disrespect	8%	44%	91	450
Violation of rules for *clothing* worn at school.	Clothing	8%	52%	87	537
Disruptive or off-task behavior in class.	Disruptive	6%	59%	66	603
Use, possession, attempt to sell or distribute *tobacco* at school.	Tobacco	6%	65%	64	667
Being *tardy* to class.	Tardy	5%	71%	57	724
Harassing, intimidating, threatening another student.	Harrassing	4%	75%	44	768
Truancy, having an unexcused absence at school.	Truancy	3%	79%	36	804
Violation of *bus* rules.	Bus	3%	82%	34	838
Fighting, attacking, deliberately harming another student.	Fighting	3%	85%	31	869
Violation of *cafeteria* rules.	Cafeteria	2%	87%	23	892
Committing an *illegal* act at school.	Illegal	1%	89%	20	912

Continued

Continued

Description	Category	Percent	Cumulative Percent	Number	Cumulative Numbers
Inappropriate display of *affection*.	Affection	1%	91%	18	930
Vandalism is the deliberate damaging of property.	Vandalism	1%	93%	17	947
Use, possession, attempt to sell or distribute, being under the influence of illegal *drugs* or the misuse of legal drugs at school.	Drugs	1%	94%	13	960
Endangering anyone else by a deliberate act at school.	Endangering	1%	95%	12	972
Violation of the closed *campus* rule. This is a *truancy*.	Campus	1%	96%	11	983
Violation of rules for driving or parking a *car* at school.	Car	0.89%	97%	9	992
Use, possession, attempt to sell or distribute, being under the influence of *alcohol* at school.	Alcohol	0.79%	98%	8	1000
Violation of *computer* and/or Internet use contracts.	Computer	0.59%	99%	6	1006
Committing a *hate* motivated offense against another student.	Hate	0.39%	99%	4	1010
Possession of a gun or other *weapon* at school.	Weapons	0.39%	99%	4	1014
Creating a false *emergency*, such as setting off a false fire alarm.	Emergency	0.20%	100%	2	1016
Totals					**1016**

third to fourth to fifth, and so on. These speakers are partially correct. One cannot compare third to third, but one can compare third to third to third to third. Trend data is accurate and the more years one has the more accurate it is. When leaders are only provided two years of data, this year and last year, the data are useless. If the scores go up, one can only say there is a 50 percent chance we were lucky and if the scores go down, one can only say there is a 50 percent chance we were unlucky. The more years of data one has, the more likely luck (the intelligence of the students) is not a factor. On the scatter diagram included in this chapter, one can easily declare that it is not luck that has increased fourth-graders' math knowledge. On the other hand, if all one was observing were the years 2003 and 2005, one would have to wonder if the difference was caused by the fact that different students were tested. That said, the cohort does provide additional valuable insight. Track the students from grade level to grade level. Our only suggestion is to label the graph according to when the students will graduate from high school: "The class of 2012," for example. This way the title does not need to change when a new set of numbers is added each year to the database.

In conclusion, there is much to be learned from studying the results (summative) data. Every leader has the same two choices in regard to the use of the data: beat up on the people with threats or use the data to gain insight for a better future. Our desire is that readers of this book will use the data suggestions to create a better future for their staffs and students.

Core Values

Managing for innovation to improve the school and create value for students and stakeholders.

Public responsibility and citizenship that goes beyond mere compliance.

Management by fact that uses performance measurement to focus on improving student learning.

Focus on results and creating value as the means to improving student learning and demonstrating accountability.

Baldrige Connection

Describe how your measurement plan includes observations and measures or indicators that are used to provide timely information to help students and faculty improve learning. Among the key factors to be addressed in assessment are ensuring appropriate comparisons among students and the relevance of assessment criteria to your mission and objectives. Differences

---

Continued

Continued

among students must be a critical consideration in the evaluation of key educational processes. In addition, assessment optimally should be related to the knowledge and skill requirements of offerings, and assessment should provide students and others with key information about what students know and are able to do.

Guiding Questions

Summative assessments are tailored to the educational offerings and program goals. In addition to these assessments, do your observations, measures, and indicators include enrollment and participation figures, student evaluations of courses and instructors, success rates, attendance rates, dropout rates, information from student counselors, advanced study rates, complaints, feedback from students and families, and formal classroom observation by faculty leaders? What key performance measures or indicators are used for the control and improvement of your learning-centered processes?

Adapted from *2005 Education Criteria for Performance Excellence.*

REFERENCES AND READING LIST

Buckingham, Marcus. 2005. *The One Thing You Need to Know.* New York: The Free Press.

Covey, Stephen. 1989. *The 7 Habits of Highly Effective People.* New York: Simon and Schuster.

From L to J Software. 2003. *Knowledge Power Software.* Scottsdale, AZ. www.knowledgepower.com.

23

Grading: How the Public Knows Schools are Disorganized

OVERVIEW

Assume you had the opportunity of a lifetime for an administrator: unlimited funding, the ability to hire the dream team, and a year to organize the school with the team in place before the students arrived. Also, the leading experts in education are available to work with the team to provide the best ideas in systems thinking, motivation, building relationships, data, evaluation, and grading practices. From this work, you would develop the policies for the school. Such a deal!

The problem is that the end result, very likely, will not work. Why? What we have described is a system of parts, or processes, and not a complete system designed to accomplish the aim of the school. Some of the parts could actually work against each other. One such example is the typical grading process. What most American schools have, in regard to grading, is a disjointed mess. Very few people agree on grading policies. Furthermore, the development, implementation, and evaluation of the school plans rarely include a discussion of grading.

Why is a grading policy an unimportant part of the school improvement plan? It is most probably because grading either is considered sacred or appears to be a constant (we have always done it this way) in the sea of change we know as education. When grading is treated as an untouchable, for either reason, grades are not likely to describe the learning that has or has not occurred. Most students have several teachers who employ multiple and varied grading practices. There is seldom any consistency or even any attempt to coordinate these grading practices. This utter lack of coordination concerning the meaning of grades is one reason society feels schools are disorganized.

How does one approach and facilitate a discussion on grades? First, grading is not the place to begin. The place to begin is with the aim of the district, school, and the subject at hand. If it were accepted, for example, that the aim was to increase success and decrease failure, then grading practices should assist leaders with this aim. The grades should indicate whether the students are successful learners or have failed to grasp the concepts for the grading period. This involves much more than a single letter grade.

Next, there is the team. When the team consists of the teacher and his or her students, then grades have a different focus. The teacher is now the coach of the team and desires for all students to win. Lloyd likes to say "feedback is the true breakfast of champions," which means that specific and immediate information on a student's performance is much more important than a grade.

An incident that illustrates the problem with grading occurred when Lloyd's son Jim was a kindergarten student. It illustrates a child's perception of grades. Jim began kindergarten when he was four and was the youngest in his class. At the end of the first week of afternoon kindergarten, Jim arrived home Friday evening with a colorful envelope securely pinned to his shirt. The note, nicely written in cursive, simply said, "Jim appears to be a little immature." Lloyd chose to ignore the note—conceding that the teacher was probably right; after all, he was four. At the end of the second week, Jim came home with a second note. This time the note, written on a large sheet of grey paper with no envelope, contained only three words, "James is immature." Being a typical parent, Lloyd asked Jim about the note and, being a typical child, Jim disavowed any knowledge of a problem. His answer was, "School is fun, I like recess." Hoping that this too would pass, Lloyd procrastinated about contacting the teacher. At the end of the third week Lloyd's phone rang at 3:00 PM with the kindergarten teacher on the other end of the line ranting that she had been teaching for twenty-some years and had never taught a child like Jim. Her instructions were to immediately come to school and discuss the issue or she was not sending Jim home! Lloyd complied and upon his arrival was asked to have a seat in an eight-inch kindergarten chair next to Jim. The teacher began with week one and displayed some blank coloring sheets with Jim's name scrawled in four-year-old script. The teacher mentioned she had sent home a note about this issue the end of the first week. After explaining that she told him he must color the sheets, she produced the second week's work. The sheet contained one color scribbled out of the lines with Jim's name again scrawled in four-year-old script. Becoming more indignant, the teacher explained she had sent a second note home at the end of that week. Next, she produced the third week's papers and having instructed Jim to use more than one color, the sheets contained two colors scribbled out of the lines with Jim's name. Finally, she held up the paper from that Friday, the one that prompted the emergency phone call. It was identical to the ones from earlier in the week with the exception of a very large red F. The irate teacher fumed that she thought the F would "shock Jim into reality." She turned to Lloyd and asked, "Do you know what he said when I showed this to him?" Lloyd, by now feeling somewhat intimidated himself, said, "no, what?" She said Jim told her it was "just a mark on a piece of paper!" The truth was that Lloyd's four-year-old had learned what grades were in just three weeks and his teacher still did not know after twenty-plus years of teaching! A grade must have more meaning to the child than simply a mark.

The standards are what students are to know and to be able to perform at the end of the course. The coach is there to assure that all students meet the standards. Grades are merely a communication device to let the students and their parents know if they are meeting standards and at what level learning is occurring. Teachers can say their aim is for all students to earn an A because their aim is for all students to learn all that is presented, explored, and discussed, and their job is to work with the students until this occurs.

What should be graded or measured? Evidence that students have met the learning standards is what is measured. Practice is not graded; evidence is graded. This means that the majority of grades are exams, projects, speeches, essays, alternative assessments, authentic assessments, and other performances. Ideally, grades should correlate perfectly with learning. A few districts where we have led the continuous improvement process are using either a dual system of reporting grades and reporting student mastery against year-end goals or have gone completely to the narrative mastery report and eliminated graded report cards. One should be able to believe, with great confidence, that a student receiving an A in a classroom has placed the content of the course into his/her long-term memory and can apply the knowledge in new situations. The student may or may not be particularly responsible when it comes to daily assignments. This information can be communicated to parents in ways other than academic grades.

Grading for success in a culture of all-time-bests (see Figure 23.1) requires that teachers realize that grade books are full of noninformation and that grades are symbols educators invented to explain their judgment on what they thought about the learning.

Regarding graded exams, the exams do not need to be on only past chapters or units. They can be exams on an entire year's curriculum, with the grading scale adjusted according to content taught. Following is a description of how some teachers are setting up their grading scale for exams.

1. Assignments aren't the outcomes.
2. Assessment requires feedback, not grades.
3. Monitor everything that is important.
4. Don't grade everything that moves.
5. Grade in pencil, not permanent ink.
6. Low performance is incomplete success.
7. Don't reward poor performance by grading it.
8. Assess for success, don't grade for selection.
9. Grade outcomes, not time blocks.
10. Chart, chart, chart!

Figure 23.1   How to grade for success in a culture of all-time-bests.

Grading Options

Option 1—For a Course with No Prerequisite Knowledge Required

Students are given a minimum of four end-of-the-year finals. Each assessment is a different version, but all are based on the course expectations provided to students the first week of class. Students are expected to answer the percentage of the exam questions that correspond to the percentage of the course taught. For example, at the end of the first quarter, students are expected to answer 25 percent of the questions correctly. A grading scale for an exam with 48 questions could look like Table 23.1 if 90 percent equals an A, and so on.

Option 2—With Course Requiring Prerequisite Knowledge

Students are informed that one-third of their grade on exams will be their knowledge of prior grade/course content and two-thirds, their knowledge of the current course. They are no longer given permission to forget the work of prior years. Students are provided, if necessary, the content expectations of prior courses. The grading scale combines the expectation of knowing 100 percent of prior-year content and the appropriate percentage of current-year content. The example shown in Table 23.2 is for an exam with 48 questions.

Table 23.1 Option 1—For a course with no prerequisite knowledge required.

Time of exam	Expectation	Grading scale
First quarter	25%—12 of 48	11 = A; 10 = B; 9 = C; 8 = D
Semester	50%—24 of 48	22 = A; 20 = B; 18 = C; 16 = D
Third quarter	75%—36 of 48	33 = A; 30 = B; 27 = C; 24 = D
End of course	100%—48 of 48	44 = A; 40 = B; 36 = C; 32 = D

Table 23.2 Option 2—With course requiring prerequisite knowledge.

Time of exam	Prior expectation	Current expectation	Grading scale
First quarter	100%—16 questions	25%—8 of 32	22 = A; 19 = B; 17 = C; 14 = D
Semester	100%—16 questions	50%—16 of 32	29 = A; 26 = B; 22 = C; 19 = D
Third quarter	100%—16 questions	75%—24 of 32	36 = A; 32 = B; 28 = C; 24 = D
End of course	100%—16 questions	100%—32 of 32	43 = A; 38 = B; 34 = C; 29 = D

Core Values

Focus on results and creating value. A school's performance measurements focus on key results.

Baldrige Connection

Describe how grades are used to create and balance value for your students and for your key stakeholders—the community, parents, employers, faculty and staff, suppliers and partners, and the public. The use of a grades as performance measures offers an effective means to communicate short- and longer-term priorities, monitor actual performance, and provide a clear basis for improving results.

Guiding Questions

How does your school evaluate student performance? Are the students' grades representative of student success?

Adapted from *2005 Education Criteria for Performance Excellence.*

24

Are the Results Ever Good Enough? Two Answers

OVERVIEW

For decades school leaders have espoused the desire for excellence in education. Educators have tried a myriad of reforms and restructuring efforts to get better, but how good do educators really want to be? Six Sigma is a practice used in many businesses to improve quality and ultimately profit. A process operating at six sigma has three defects per million opportunities. In the opinion of some, this is good enough. If we process 1,000,000 checks with three errors, that is good enough. If we manufacture 1,000,000 phones and only three do not work, that is good enough. There is a whole industry built up around Six Sigma training in industry, with a few interested school districts. If six sigma were easy, the Six Sigma industry could not thrive.

Below are some other numbers to help us think about "good enough." What is excellence or lack thereof? Is 60 percent good enough? We allow students to move to the next level with a D. Is 70 percent or 80 percent or even 90 percent? Let's consider 99 percent accuracy (just one percent error). If we consider this good enough there would be:

- At least 250,000 incorrect drug prescriptions written each year

- More than 30,000 newborns dropped by doctors and nurses each year

- Unsafe drinking water at least four days of the year

- No electricity, water, or heat for nearly 15 minutes every day

- No telephone service or cellular service for more than two hours each week

- No television transmission for 10 hours each month

- Two long or short landings at most major airports every day

Let's consider 99.9 percent accuracy (one tenth of one percent error). If we consider this good enough there would be:

- 26,000 botched surgeries each year

- 175 million checks deducted from wrong accounts

- 75 billion misplaced phone calls by telephone services

- 2.5 million books shipped with wrong covers

- 6600 commercial airline crashes each year

In some schools today, we have become so concerned about political correctness that we have failed to maintain high expectations for student performance. In fact, students have learned that what we accept is really what we expect. The result has become a deluge of mediocre work. We would rather give a bad, but passing, grade rather than give the assignment back and expect a better product. There is a cost to our failure to educate America's children:

- Over $300 billion annually for formal and informal training

- Over $50 billion annually for welfare programs dominated by school dropouts

- $25 billion in additional welfare costs due to teen pregnancies

- $35 billion each year in lost productivity

- $280 billion in lost earnings and taxes over the lifetime of each year's school dropouts (Federal Training Register, 2000)

IMPLEMENTATION STEPS

All this and America continues to spend $2 billion a day to educate its youth. How good is good enough? Caroline, Lloyd, and Lee have worked in many districts that assumed good enough was meeting minimum standards and being identified as off the at-risk list. Why have so many failed? Here are a few of our conjectures:

- No clear aim

- All talk—no walk

- Lack of knowledge and research by teachers and principals

- Excuses: It's not our fault, it's society's

- Lack of resources

- Outdated or no technology

- Poorly developed curriculum

- Ineffective staff development

- A belief that there is a lack of a need for change

- Don't rock the boat, we still have some successful graduates

- Rut—100-plus-year-old paradigm

- Board, administration, and staff turnover

- Government bureaucracy

- Union mentality

- Staff goals different from organization

- Not my job

TOOLS

How can you, as a school leader, ratchet up the levels of performance in your school(s)? Begin by getting parents involved—share with them the learning goals and essential facts to be mastered for the year, ensure that students have a maximum amount of time on task where they are academically engaged and not given permission to forget. Always focus on learning from a curriculum that is clearly defined and important to the learner, lead relentlessly, have high expectations that are supported by working on the various processes of the system, monitor and report student achievement via weekly formative classroom assessments and charting to display results, provide a safe place for learning and use quality tools to continuously improve. To make this work there are a few requirements:

- Plan your work and work your plan

- Do today's work today

- You must care and show it
- You must be sensitive to other people's needs and feelings
- Make good things happen
- Take necessary risks
- Work at team-building
- Give credit to faculty, staff, and students if things go well
- Take responsibility if things go wrong
- Practice systems thinking
- Celebrate all-time-bests

A few things to remember:

- You can't be effective if you're always behind your desk
- Actions speak louder than words
- You catch more flies with honey than you do with vinegar
- Don't say yes if you don't mean it
- Don't say no if you can't back it up
- Providing the best possible educational opportunities is the bottom line

Finally, achieving excellence must be a journey of continuous improvement, reaching for all-time-bests.

25

Personal Growth and Personal Learning: Invest in Yourself

OVERVIEW

Teachers generally are the focus of professional development, not the administrator. However, an underestimation of the importance of professional development for the principal would be a serious mistake. The principal should be the school's lead learner. Two examples of improving personal learning are staying current with the literature of the field and reflecting on personal leadership action.

The principal in an urban area is often afforded districtwide general professional development opportunities by central office. On the other hand, a principal in a small or rural district may have limited opportunities for formal professional development. It is important to include self-directed professional development as one of the primary methods of improving leadership and instructional practices.

Rebore stresses that a principal's professional development should be relevant to his or her job, ongoing and personalized, flexible for change, convenient, aligned with the district's policies, and supported by adequate funding. "It is advantageous to write down such personalized programs in a document that includes a personal needs assessment and a plan of action" (2004, 181). In an analysis of the professional development habits of three outstanding principals, Fleming observed that the administrators were "active in their own learning and are open to new ideas" (1999, 1). Not only did these principals immerse themselves in new literature and workshops, but they also applied their new learning to their schools.

A school building leader is expected to lead by example. The principal's attitude toward professional development sets the tone for the building.

It is essential to be an active participant in any staff development, especially training for a major reform initiative. Administrative absence sends the message that the training and initiative are unimportant. Administrative presence states more than words that the initiative is important. It is also imperative that the administrator have a thorough understanding of the reform. Attending the teacher training is one way to develop such an understanding.

A major portion of personal growth should be from articles in professional journals. Due to the wide variety of demands on their time and the interruptions experienced by a principal every day, reading and reflection should be regularly scheduled. If it's not on your planner, it won't get done. This can be an opportunity to abstract and summarize articles that are important and relevant to achieving the aim of the school. Collaborating on research efforts with other administrators and teachers allows more information to be discovered and disseminated.

EXAMPLE

Lloyd was once assigned the task of converting a junior high school into a middle school, with seven months to prepare the teachers for the change. Knowing that teachers will resist change if they see no benefit for their students and themselves, an informational campaign was initiated that included researching, reading, and abstracting a journal article each week. The abstracts were copied onto 3×5 cards and put in the teachers' mailboxes each Monday. They were called "hit the can cards" referring to the fact that they could be read before landing in the trash can. A few copies of the complete article were left in the teacher's lounge and several teachers read them regularly. A follow-up discussion of the articles was a focus during faculty meetings.

This served as one form of professional development for administrator and staff.

IMPLEMENTATION STEPS

Self-Directed Personal Growth Program

A personal growth program should complement an administrator's educational preparation with professional development that fills gaps and addresses weaknesses. The possibilities for professional learning are vast, and reach well beyond what can be addressed in this book.

Steps in developing a personal growth program include:

1. *Plan.* Create a self-directed professional development plan. Identify goals for professional growth and how these goals might be achieved. Organize a time line and activities.

2. *Portfolio.* Create a professional portfolio and document learning experiences.

3. *Administrator performance conference.* Utilize the professional growth portfolio during the formal evaluation conference as evidence of a self-driven plan of improvement. This will provide an opportunity for discussion of both achievement and suggestions for future growth activities.

Example of Time Line and Activities

August/September

Complete personal needs assessment.

- Review the concerns you have about your knowledge, skills, and abilities

- Connect your concerns with the ISSLC Standards, ELLC Standards or state administrative standards

- Identify manageable goals that can be addressed during the year

Design an initial professional development plan. Some examples of learning topics and activities include:

Managing learning

Supervising and evaluating teaching

Finance

Personal productivity

Professional organizations

Social and legal issues

Classroom management

Student-centered learning environments

Addressing individual needs and differences

Data-driven decision making

Curriculum

Instruction

Professional development

Professional reading

Student assessment

Technology use

Internet survival skills

Understanding contemporary issues

September to April

Use at least four self-directed strategies to enact the professional development plan. Create a professional portfolio to organize artifacts of learning related to professional development goals (for example, conference materials, articles, pictures, newspaper clippings, seminar agendas, workshop notes, and university course work). Integrate learnings and materials that contribute to professional development. Reflect on the meaning of activities and experiences as each activity or professional development topic is completed. Document both the progress toward goals and the learning that occurred. Revise the learning goals and strategies as necessary.

Immediately after Spring Break

Organize the portfolio to highlight professional growth. Select artifacts that help tell the story of your professional growth for the year. Summarize all professional growth.

Carry Out Your Plan

To achieve the goal, select a variety of activities. For example, if the professional development plan highlights learning more about teacher evaluation, the plan might include: consulting the professional literature and reading several articles, attending a workshop on performance evaluation, watching a video, and presenting a workshop yourself.

TOOLS

According to Peterson and Cosner, school districts and principals can use the following four approaches to enhance school principals' opportunities to learn from experience:

1. Structured interactions with the superintendent

2. Structured interactions with experienced administrators

3. Mentors and coaches

4. Customized collaborative ventures with universities or professional development organizations "using case-based and problem-based learning" (2005, 30)

Core Values

Organizational and personal learning that is directed not only toward better educational programs and services, but also toward being more flexible, adaptive, and responsive to the needs of students and stakeholders.

Baldrige Connection

Faculty and staff success depends increasingly on having opportunities for personal learning and practicing new skills. Schools invest in personal learning through education, training, and other opportunities for continuing growth and development.

Personal learning can result in (1) more satisfied and versatile faculty and staff who stay with your school, (2) organizational cross-functional learning, (3) the building of your school's knowledge assets, and (4) an improved environment for innovation.

Guiding Questions

How does your school show evidence of learning? Processes should include evaluation and improvement cycles, as well as the potential for breakthrough change. How are process improvements shared with other appropriate units of the school to enable organizational learning? At what level do faculty and staff participate in professional development opportunities? How do school leaders work to eliminate disincentives for groups and individuals to sustain these important, learning-focused professional development activities?

Adapted from *2005 Education Criteria for Performance Excellence.*

RESOURCES AND READING LIST

Fleming, Grace, and Tara Leo. 1999. "Principals and Teachers: Continuous Learners." [Electronic version]. *Southwest Educational Development Laboratory* 7, no 2: 1–8.

Fullan, Michael. 2001. *Leading in a Culture of Change.* New York: John Wiley & Sons.

Peterson, Kent. 2002. "The Professional Development of Principals: Innovations and Opportunities." [Electronic version]. *Educational Administrative Quarterly* 38, no. 2: 213–32.

Peterson, Kent, and Shelley Cosner. 2005. "Teaching Your Principal." [Electronic version]. *Journal of Staff Development* 26, no. 2: 28–32.

Rebore, Ronald W. 2004. *Human Resources Administration in Education,* 7th ed. Boston: Pearson Education.

LINKS

ASCD—http//:www.ascd.org
Center for Creative Leadership—http//:www.ccl.org/leadership/index.aspx
National Association of Elementary School Principals—http//:www.naesp.org
National Association of Secondary School Principals—http//:www.nassp.org
National Staff Development Council—http//:www.nsdc.org
Southern Regional Education Board—http//:www.sreb.org
The Institute for Educational Leadership—http//:www.iel.org
The Principals' Partnership—http//:www.principalspartnership.com
University Council for Educational Administration—http//:www.ucea.org
WestEd—http//:www.wested.org

26

Efficiency and Productivity: Wise Use of Both Money and Time

OVERVIEW

How would we know if schools were more productive? It is not as easy to describe as it is in business. A business is more productive if it decreases expenses and increases profit. If a business produces five percent more product with the same number of employees, then it is five percent more productive. Schools are not used to measuring productivity; maybe they should.

How would we know if a school district was more productive? At the very least a school system would be more productive if it produced more high school graduates with the same number of staff members. One could also use advanced placement (AP) exams passed as a measure of productivity. The school system had a five percent increase in AP exam passage with no increase in budget; productivity increased.

Efficiency is an aspect of productivity. When school systems use their resources efficiently, it simply means they are used without wasting them. How are resources wasted?

1. Teaching children to read that didn't make it in kindergarten, first grade, or fall of second grade.

2. A student failing a year or a course. Costs are doubled, as the same instructional costs must be paid twice.

3. Students are habitually absent or tardy. Instructional time is wasted reteaching.

4. Purchasing a textbook series that is not organized K–12. When different companies publish for elementary, middle, and high school, the work is not coordinated; much is unnecessarily retaught, which wastes time. For example, the publisher of fifth-grade U.S. history, eighth-grade U.S. history, and 11th-grade U.S. history texts are often different, thus schools are not going to use their time efficiently.

This chapter is about leaders accepting the responsibility to make schools more efficient. The goal is not to build up a huge bank account for the school district, but to become more productive by offering more music, more library services, more advanced courses, more field trips, and so on.

Efficiency is about the long term: how can we cut down on time wasters and money wasters? The time and money wasters do not go away. However, with great effort they can be reduced. Ideally, schools would spend 100 percent of their money on learning. Buildings would be free, no time would be wasted on building referendums, there would be no payroll costs, insurance costs would be paid by somebody else, there would be no vandalism, nobody would get hurt on the job, and no time would be wasted on students misbehaving. Nirvana is not going to occur. However, reducing waste can be done. This is the first step in becoming more productive. Table 26.1 provides a starting place for school leaders to calculate the cost, in time and money, for activities that do not increase student learning.

Collecting the baseline data will be a year-long task, with everybody involved in creating a list of tasks that are not directly related to learning. Nobody should consider the tasks unrelated to learning as unimportant and think they are not valued. The point is not importance or unimportance; it is productivity. If the dumpsters are not emptied, we'll have big problems. However, if we can decrease the cost of dumpster emptying by one dollar per student per year, we are more efficient. And if the one dollar is spent well, educators can become more productive. Students can not learn in chaos; discipline is essential. Increased productivity, however, would mean that the assistant principal is spending 600 hours per year on discipline rather than the former 1200 hours per year.

Every school and district office needs two charts: one for money and one for time. Lists are compiled and edited. People are keeping data. How many hours per year are spent on payroll? If a school district cuts payroll errors by 75 percent (efficiency), they can then handle an increase in employees with no additional people in the payroll office. Again, if the money saved by not adding to the payroll office is spent wisely, then the school district has a chance to be more productive.

Table 26.1   Productivity measures.

Noninstructional responsibility	Measurement metric
Discipline referrals to office	Hours per year
Taking and reporting attendance	Hours per year
Payroll	Hours per year
Emptying trash dumpsters	Dollars per student per year
Substitutes for employees at jury duty	Dollars per student per year
Mailing transcripts of moved students	Dollars per student per year
Labor negotiations	Dollars per student per year
Home to school transportation	Dollars per student per year
Preparation for school board meetings	Hours per year
Workers compensation insurance	Dollars per student per year
Liability insurance	Dollars per student per year
Reteaching courses students failed	Dollars per student per year
Remedial courses	Dollars per student per year
Attendance at required meetings not for instruction	Dollars per student per year
Time at meetings not related to learning	Hours per year
Time spent enrolling new students	Hours per year
Providing data to state departments of education	Dollars per student per year

Once the lists are compiled, they need to be cut and pasted for each successive school year. The data are then recorded on an annual basis. The lists must also be sorted from most money to least money and most hours to least hours with a *y*-axis scale. By drawing a line from each item to its location on the succeeding year's scale, an observer can see where the school district has become more efficient.

An example with one listing follows to illustrate the point. The "$" column is cost per student per year. Obviously, publishing the data annually will not increase efficiency. It is the work all through the year that creates the year-end savings. For each measure of efficiency, somebody has to "own" the improvement process. Who owns dumpster costs? Payroll costs? Somebody must "own" each efficiency measure and work all year for improvement. Some measures might be daily, such as minutes of instructional time lost to tardiness and student disruptive behavior, some could be weekly, and some monthly. Vandalism is one that could be a monthly total in most locales. Time spent in board meeting preparation is probably a monthly number.

EXAMPLES

In Jenks, Oklahoma, public schools (2006 Malcom Baldrige Award Winner), Lee was shown the blueprint room for all district schools. Why is this so important? When something needs repair, the people responsible for the repair often need building blueprints. Time wasted attempting to locate the blueprint is a lack of efficiency. In Jenks, any blueprint can be located in one or two minutes. The blueprints are cataloged in one binder, numbered, and filed in a logical system; the blueprint is located almost instantly. Lee also was shown graphs depicting less money spent each month on broken glass caused by rock-throwing lawn mowers. The food services department tracks Workers Comp claims caused by slippery, wet floors in the kitchen. Tufte's table-graphic simply adds a line to corresponding data to turn a simple table into a valuable graph (see Figure 26.1).

One final note: productivity for an entire state is the cost per high school graduate. Divide the total cost of K–12 education in your state by the number of high school graduates for this figure.

$ per student per year	Line item	2005	2006	2007
100				
90				
80				
70				
60				
50				
40				
30				
20	Empty dumpster	$12.35 ⇨	$11.47 ⇨	$9.85
10				
0				

Figure 26.1   Table-graphic for budget efficiency.

Core Values

Management by fact that uses performance measurement to focus on improving student learning.

Focus on results and creating value as the means to improving student learning and increasing productivity, effectiveness, and efficiency.

Baldrige Connection

Summarize your school's key operational performance results that contribute to opportunities for enhanced learning and to the improvement of organizational productivity and effectiveness. Segment your results by program, service, and offering, and disaggregate by student demographics as appropriate. Include appropriate comparative data.

Guiding Questions

How do you incorporate productivity and other efficiency and effectiveness factors into the design of curriculum and instruction? How do you implement these processes to ensure that they meet design requirements? What are your current levels and trends in key measures or indicators of productivity, effectiveness, and efficiency?

Adapted from *2005 Education Criteria for Performance Excellence.*

RESOURCES AND READING LIST

Tufte, Edward R. 2001. *The Visual Display of Quantitative Information,* 2nd ed. Cheshire, CT: Graphics Press.

27

No Child Left Behind (or Other Mandated Change): Do It Right

HISTORY

Currently, the No Child Left Behind Act of 2001 is the national mandate driving many decisions in education. This legislation was signed into law by President George W. Bush on January 8, 2002. It is the reauthorization of the Elementary and Secondary Education Act (ESEA) of 1965. Some of the major provisions of the act, as stated by the U.S. Department of Education (2005, Overview) are: Accountability for Results, Creating Flexibility at the State and Local Levels, Expanding Options for Parents of Children from Disadvantaged Backgrounds, Ensuring Every Child Can Read with Reading First, Strengthening Teacher Quality, Confirming Progress, and Promoting English Proficiency. To ensure that these occur, the following expectations have been included: setting higher education standards, annual testing of children to measure progress toward achieving the higher standards, analysis of the test data annually to ensure that students are progressing, and rewards (and penalties) aimed at schools where students make (or do not make) adequate yearly progress (AYP). (The K–12, 1–2).

In actuality, No Child Left Behind addresses title programs, with Title I being the major component of the initiative, as indicated by the fact that 96 of the 670 pages of legislation address Title I. The major difference in this ESEA legislation is that the requirements affect all schools and students, not just those specified under title programs. At the federal level, the penalties attached to schools who fail to meet AYP are directed only at Title I schools. However, states are required to set sanctions for the non–Title I schools.

No Child Left Behind is the most specific federal mandate for education to date. There are many who are critical of this legislation. There are also those who support the act. This is true of any mandate. Therefore, this is not a discussion of the merits of the bill, but ideas on how to successfully implement a systemic mandated change while building a culture of continuous improvement and all-time-bests.

OVERVIEW

An administrator, whether for the district or a school, who is faced with a mandated initiative has two basic choices, support the initiative or criticize the initiative. There is no room for the negative at the school level with an initiative of this nature since it will not change the facts of the mandated change. The leader will set the tone for the success of the initiative by the public face they present. According to Whittaker, "When an administrator sneezes, the whole building catches a cold" (2002, 30). This applies doubly to the mandated initiative. Therefore, if administrators want an initiative to succeed, mandated or not, they must publicly support the initiative enthusiastically.

A "can do" attitude is necessary from a critical mass to reach these goals. There may be complaints and "our students can't" statements. The administrator should allow a brief discussion, then refocus the group with the statement "This is what is; what are we going to do about it!"

Administrators must learn everything they can about the initiative. In order to do this, data must be evaluated to determine the district or school's current standing in the areas that will be measured. "Where are we now?" "What do we need to do to reach the established goal?" These are questions that must be addressed. Data will focus the work.

Another area to address is how the mandate fits into the aim, vision, mission, beliefs, and philosophy of the district. If there are mismatches, ways to address these must be determined. One example, expressed by many, is the frustration with standardized testing and the idea that a one-time test should not be used to determine a student's success for the year. This discussion should be saved for conversations with peers. Testing has been a part of the evaluation of students and districts for some time and there is no indication the trend will change in the near future, so it is really a futile discussion at the building level. There are two ways to address this problem. First, make sure test results are not the focus of the district. Second, make sure there are multiple methods in place to evaluate student success.

It is sometimes difficult for districts that have been labeled at-risk to think of anything but the end test results. Focusing on the test does not improve student performance; focusing on the standards, determining the essential information to be learned, using a variety of data as information to inform decisions about curriculum, teaching and learning, providing extra tutoring for low-performing students, providing opportunities to apply the knowledge at higher cognitive levels, and celebrating success improve test scores. However, the goal is increased student learning. Districts or schools that focus on the test often lose focus on learning after the test date has passed. Districts or schools that focus on increased student learning maintain focus until the final bell in the spring. Since a school must test at least 95 percent of students, including special education and limited language learners, special attention must be paid to these subgroups.

The No Child Left Behind Act does not just include testing as the one final indicator of AYP. The other mandated AYP indicators are the graduation rate for secondary schools and at least one noninstructional indicator at the elementary level. Other indicators are set at the state level, as well as the benchmarks for each indicator. What occurs in one state does not necessarily occur in the next since the states set many of the AYP indicators.

IMPLEMENTATION STEPS

Utilize the plan–do–study–act improvement model to organize your implementation. This format can be used to implement any new program.

Plan

- Study state requirements for NCLB

- Gather supporting data

- Chart the data for clearer understanding

- Determine gaps and areas of success

- Plan first meeting with teachers (This should be a very organized meeting while maintaining the flexibility needed to allow input by everyone.)

- Gather all involved for planning meeting

- Celebrate areas of success

- Utilize discussion strategies to address gaps (This is essential; most teachers must have buy-in to the solutions before they implement the plan. Also, make sure every teacher has a voice in the planning.)

- Establish a plan of action (Include a time line and those responsible for each step.)

- Adjust the schedule so teachers can meet regularly to evaluate progress

- Focus on the positives while improving the negatives

Do

- Implement the plan

- Graph results to monitor successes or gaps

- Teacher groups should meet regularly to evaluate the data (Keep notes concerning what worked and what needs to be adjusted for the next year.)

- Celebrate the successes with students

- Include students in the discussion of how to increase success

- Teach or review test-taking skills with students

- Focus students toward success in the weeks prior to testing (Students work off of the cues teachers send. A positive attitude and focus on a "can do" attitude all year, especially prior to testing, can increase test scores.)

- Monitor and chart student attendance, discipline, or other areas of concern

- Focus on the positives while improving the negatives

Study

- Utilize the data from the state to determine areas of growth, decline, or stability

- Evaluate the plan

- Adjust for areas of concern

Act

- Internalize the processes that worked

- Repeat the plan–do–study–act cycle

FURTHER EXAMPLES

One example of a district that has used the continuous improvement process to increase performance is Jenks Public Schools in Jenks, Oklahoma. This district has consistently performed at high levels. They were awarded the Malcolm Baldrige National Quality Award in Spring 2006. The district's focus has been on excellence in five areas that they call the five A's—*academics, arts, activities, athletics, and attitude.* More information concerning this district can be found at the following links, which are to the district Web site and the Baldrige Award information.

http://www.jenksps.org/

http://www.jenksps.org/baldrige/index.html

Core Values

Learning-centered education that places the focus of education on learning and the real needs of students and developing the fullest potential of all students.

Social responsibility and citizenship that not only meets all local, state, and federal laws and regulatory requirements, but that treats these and related requirements as opportunities for improvement "beyond mere compliance."

Baldrige Connection

Describe how your school builds and manages its knowledge assets to ensure equity and adequacy of learning for all children. Describe how your school measures, analyzes, aligns, reviews, and improves student performance data and information at all levels and in all parts of your school. Describe how your school ensures the quality and availability of needed data and information for faculty and staff, students and stakeholders, and suppliers and partners. Describe how your school maintains a positive school and classroom climate that contributes to the well-being, satisfaction, and motivation of all children.

Guiding Questions

What are your school's main educational programs, offerings, and services? What are the delivery mechanisms used to provide your educational programs, offerings, and services to students? What is your organizational culture? What are your stated aim, vision, mission, and values? What is your faculty and staff profile? What are their education levels; are they highly qualified? What is the regulatory environment under which your school

---

Continued

Continued

operates? What are the mandated federal, state, and local standards, curricula, programs, and assessments, applicable occupational health and safety regulations, accreditation requirements, administrator and teacher certification requirements, and environmental and financial regulations? How do you maintain an overall organizational focus on performance improvement, including organizational learning? How do you achieve systematic evaluation and improvement of key processes?

Adapted from *2005 Education Criteria for Performance Excellence.*

RESOURCES AND READING LIST

K–12 Principal's Guide to No Child Left Behind. 2003. Alexandria, VA: National Association of Elementary Principals and National Association of Secondary Principals.

Whittaker, Todd. 2002. *What Great Principals Do Differently: Fifteen Things That Matter Most.* Larchmont, NY: Eye on Education.

LINKS

http://www.ed.gov/nclb/overview/intro/factsheet.html
http://www.ed.gov/print/nclb/overview/intro/guide/guide.html
http://www.ed.gov/policy/elsec/leg/esea02/index.html

28

Developing New Leaders: Is the Current Leader Effective?

OVERVIEW

It is no surprise to those in education that a large percentage of school administrators are currently retiring or will be in the near future (Frankel and Hayot 2001). This leaves open a gap in school leadership that needs to be filled if our schools are to be effective. Fullan (2003) believes that a key characteristic of effective leaders is their ability to leave leaders behind who are capable of continuing the reform. The source of this leadership potential is in every principal's building: the teachers. Teacher leadership comes in several forms: department heads, mentors, club advisors, teaching teams, and coaches; some teachers choose to transition to administration.

A key to fostering leadership potential in teachers is to empower them. This means that the principal, instead of mandating teacher responsibility, gives the faculty more control over the decisions that affect their development and the vision of the school. According to Cotton, "Research repeatedly finds that when principals empower their staffs through sharing leadership and decision-making authority with them, everyone benefits, including students" (2003, 21). Sergiovanni and Starratt (1998) suggest that the principal's role in fostering teacher leadership is to support their actions and create a trusting relationship that encourages collegiality and mentoring of other teachers. Ubben, Hughes, and Norris (2004) stress that teachers also need to be given the opportunity to develop to their full potential. This is achieved through collegiality, being presented with responsibility, and receiving productive feedback to complement accomplishments and determine areas for growth.

IMPLEMENTATION STEPS

1. Define teacher leadership

   a. Understand formal and informal teacher leadership

      i. Formal roles are assigned authority

2. Be comfortable with teacher leaders

   a. See teacher leaders as assets

   b. Understand that you (the principal) may have to change certain behaviors when teachers are leading

3. Encourage teachers to become leaders

   a. All teachers should be encouraged to become leaders

   b. Create a culture where teacher leadership is appreciated

4. Help teachers develop leadership skills

   a. Provide professional development experiences

   b. Facilitate on-the-job training

5. Provide feedback

   a. Be specific

   b. Emphasize what was done well first

   c. Limit constructive feedback

TOOLS

Mike Schmoker, author of *Results: The Key to Continuous School Improvement,* suggests that teacher leadership should be formalized in the following ways:

1. *Designate—and cultivate—talented teacher leaders at every school.* Ideally, they should be both competent and respected members of the faculty. Department heads or the equivalent should be chosen on this basis rather than on seniority or popularity.

2. *Pay them a reasonable stipend. Leadership is not free.* Teacher leaders should be given at least a modest stipend. Hour for hour, their compensation should certainly be no less than what we pay coaches.

3. *Provide them with release time.* Find ways to relieve them with substitute teachers or by finding creative ways to give them a few hours off whenever possible. Even modest amounts of regularly scheduled time can go a long way.

4. *Include them in administrative training.* Teacher leaders become a principal's most valued ally and interpreter of effective structures and methods.

5. *Involve the faculty in their selection.* Invite teachers and administrators at the district level to establish results-oriented criteria and expectations for these positions. Then on the basis of the criteria, ask school faculties to help select the teacher leaders, perhaps for a designated term (Schmoker 1999, 117).

Core Values

Valuing faculty, staff, and partners by leadership who is not only dependent upon but committed to the knowledge, skills, innovative creativity, and motivation of its workforce.

Visionary leadership. Your school's senior leaders should set directions and create a student-focused, learning-oriented climate, clear and visible values, and high expectations.

Baldrige Connection

Describe how staff development, compensation, career progression, and related workforce practices enable faculty and staff to achieve leadership roles.

Describe how faculty and staff education, training, and development address leadership development.

Guiding Questions

How do you motivate faculty and staff to develop and utilize their full potential? How does your school use formal and informal mechanisms to help faculty and staff attain job- and career-related development and learning objectives?

How do you accomplish effective succession planning for leadership and supervisory positions? How do you manage effective career progression for all faculty and staff throughout the school? How do you identify characteristics and skills needed by potential leaders? How do you recruit and hire educational leaders?

Adapted from *2005 Education Criteria for Performance Excellence.*

RESOURCES AND READING LIST

Bruckner, K. G., and James O. McDowelle. 2000. "Developing Teacher Leaders: Providing Encouragement, Opportunities, and Support." [Electronic version]. *NASSP Bulletin* 84, no. 6: 35–41.

Cotton, Kathleen. 2003. *Principals and Student Achievement: What the Research Says.* Alexandria, VA: ASCD.

Frankel, Marc, and Patricia Hayot. 2001. "School Leadership at a Crossroads." [Electronic version]. *Independent School* 60, no. 2: 68–78.

Fullan, Michael. 2003. *The Moral Imperative of School Leadership.* Thousand Oaks, CA: Corwin Press.

Schmoker, Michael. 1999. *Results: The Key to Continuous School Improvement.* Alexandria, VA: ASCD.

Sergiovanni, T. J., and R. J. Starratt. 1998. *Supervision: A Redefinition.* Boston: McGraw-Hill.

Ubben, G. C., L. W. Hughes, and C. J. Norris. 2004. *The Principal: Creative Leadership for Excellence in Schools.* Boston: Pearson Education.

LINKS

Teacher Leader Network: http://www.teacherleaders.org/links.html

Teachers Network Leadership Institute: http://www.teachersnetwork.org/tnpi/index.htm

29

Baldrige in Schools: Batting 1.000

OVERVIEW

Achieving performance excellence in education is a challenge to many institutions as senior leaders attempt to deal with a range of issues from advances in information technology to decreases in financial support. Implementing the Baldrige Criteria for Education can assist in building and sustaining performance excellence in areas that are critical to the success of a school organization. Success requires the knowledge, skills, and tools essential for designing and implementing a continuous improvement program. Each chapter of this book provides the reader with information, examples, practices, or connections for determining appropriate Baldrige approach and deployment strategies to aid the school leader in attaining performance excellence.

The education version of the Baldrige Criteria was created in the mid-1990s as a framework for understanding and improving school performance and student learning. The Criteria provide the basis for assessment and feedback to educational organizations and create the foundation for continuous improvement. The criteria have four primary purposes:

- To help improve the results, capabilities, and practices of a school or district

- To share best practices and facilitate communication among educational organizations

- To serve as a working tool for understanding and improving performance and for guiding planning and opportunities for learning

- To help educational organizations use an aligned approach to performance management

The Baldrige process:

- Is not dogmatic or regulatory

- Supports a systems approach to school- and districtwide goal alignment

- Supports an aim-based process to analyze the efficacy of a schooling organization and to develop a continuous improvement plan from that analysis

The Baldrige Criteria are constructed on a set of unified core values that characterize high-performing organizations and are evident in the best schools in the nation. All of the core values are connected to the fundamental need to engage students in the learning process.

The 11 core values as listed in the 2005 Education Criteria are:

Visionary Leadership

Learning-Centered Education

Organizational and Personal Learning

Valuing Faculty, Staff, and Partners

Agility

Focus on the Future

Managing for Innovation

Management by Fact

Social Responsibility

Focus on Results and Creating Value

Systems Perspective (Baldrige 2006, 1)

While schools can identify a set of core values, what the employees of those schools do with them separates the excelling schools from the average and mediocre schools. Believing and practicing the core values of Baldrige as outlined in the education criteria can enhance the capacity of the school to dramatically impact student achievement. Core values define what a district considers essential. The mission, vision, policies, and strategies are usually dynamic, requiring regular review, but the enduring core values remain intact. They mold and control the everyday decisions and actions of the school leaders, teachers, and staff.

The Baldrige core values are personified in criteria found in seven categories:

Leadership

Strategic Planning

Student/Stakeholder Focus

Information and Analysis

Faculty/Staff Focus

Process Management

Results (Baldrige 2006, 11)

The reason to study the Baldrige process is simple: to get better results. We have included references to the Baldridge Criteria in each chapter of this book in order to help leaders make connections between various elements of successful leadership and Baldrige. We have also placed this chapter on Baldridge last because our aim is better schools through better leadership. Our aim is not to assist others in earning the Baldridge Award. Nevertheless, because the Baldridge Criteria are extremely well designed and are being updated on a regular basis, leaders need to understand the power of Baldridge.

There are numerous resources available to assist school leaders to deploy Baldrige in education. The design is to help educators improve the quality of student learning and the effectiveness of their classrooms, schools, and districts. Fortunately, educators have a variety of resources to help them shorten the cycle time between learning about continuous improvement and implementing these principles effectively.

RESOURCES AND READING LIST

Baldrige National Quality Program. 2006. *2006 Educational Criteria for Performance Excellence*. Milwaukee: American Society for Quality.

LINKS

Baldrige Award application forms: http://www.quality.nist.gov/
    Award_Application.htm
Baldrige National Quality Program: http://www.quality.nist.gov/
Jenks, Oklahoma, public schools (2006 Baldridge Award winner):
    http://www.jenksps.org/Baldrige/Index.html
BiE IN (Baldrige in Education Initiative): http://www.biein.org/
American Society for Quality: http://www.asq.org/
Improving Student Achievement: http://www.apqc.org/education/student/
Koalaty Kids: http://www.koalatykid.org/
Strengthening Quality in Schools (SQS): http://www.sandia.gov/sqs/
From L to J Consulting Group: http://www.fromltoj.com

Appendix A
Teacher Feedback Scale

Teacher Feedback Scale
Student Form B (Grades 3–6)

Name of Teacher _____ School _____ Date _____

Instructions: These statements will be used to help your teacher know what students think. Your views are important. Please circle the number which best represents your view.

1. *No,* I have not seen this behavior or sensed this attitute by my teacher.

2. *Sometimes,* I have seen this behavior or sensed this attitute by my teacher.

3. *Yes,* I have seen this behavior or sensed this attitude by my teacher.

My Teacher	No	Sometimes	Yes
1. Is a happy person	1	2	3
2. Looks at me as an important student	1	2	3
3. Helps me to like myself better.	1	2	3
4. Helps me look at the good in situations	1	2	3
5. Is fair	1	2	3
6. Is proud of my accomplishments	1	2	3

Continued

Continued

My Teacher	No	Sometimes	Yes
7. Listens to what I have to say.	1	2	3
8. Really likes me	1	2	3
9. Likes and accepts me as a person.	1	2	3
10. Tells interesting and funny stories	1	2	3
11. Is easy to understand	1	2	3
12. Is a person I like	1	2	3
13. Really encourages me to care about my classmates.	1	2	3
14. Laughs when funny things happen in class	1	2	3
My Teacher			
15. Comes to class prepared to teach	1	2	3
16. Knows a lot about many things.	1	2	3
17. Grades and gets my assignments back to me fast	1	2	3
18. Understands my strengths and weaknesses	1	2	3
19. Helps me organize my work in class	1	2	3
20. Keeps trying to learn more	1	2	3
21. Follows through on promises	1	2	3
22. Treats students as individuals	1	2	3
My Teacher			
23. Remains calm even when things go badly	1	2	3
24. Shows excitement while teaching.	1	2	3
25. Will change plans to meet my needs	1	2	3
26. Likes to try new ways to help me learn.	1	2	3
27. Takes time to understand the views of other students	1	2	3
28. Shares with us materials that are interesting	1	2	3
29. Is open to my ideas.	1	2	3
30. Has many good ideas.	1	2	3

Index